A Guide to International Monetary Reform

A Guide to International Monetary Reform

George N. Halm

Lexington Books
D. C. Heath and Company
Lexington, Massachusetts
Toronto   London

Library of Congress Cataloging in Publication Data

Halm, George Nikolaus, 1901–
   A guide to international monetary reform.

   Includes index.
   1. International finance.   2. Balance of payments.
3. Foreign exchange.   I. Title.
HG3881.H26   332.4'5   74–28969
ISBN 0–669–98061–7

Published simultaneously in Canada

Printed in the United States of America

International Standard Book Number: 0–669–98061–7

Library of Congress Catalog Card Number: 74–28969

Contents

Preface

Thirty years ago I wrote a book called *International Monetary Cooperation,* which reviewed the discussions that led to the Agreement of Bretton Woods and the creation of the International Monetary Fund. The international payments system which was then inaugurated worked reasonably well, especially when compared with the situation that prevailed before World War II. More recently, however, repeated international monetary crises and widespread floating of exchange rates have shown that the Bretton Woods arrangements must be reformed. The needed improvement of the system has been the subject of many discussions inside and outside of the International Monetary Fund. In June 1974 a committee of the Board of Governors of the Fund published an *Outline of Reform* that indicates the direction in which the system could evolve. The present volume is intended as an introduction to, and a critical commentary of, the Fund's reform proposals; it emphasizes that the present difficulties can be overcome only through much greater flexibility of exchange rates.

A Guide to International Monetary Reform

1

The Core of the International-Payments Problem

International payments could be as easy as domestic payments if we could always convert dollars freely into other currencies at permanently fixed exchange rates. International-payments problems stem from the fact that free convertibility can be combined with fixed exchange rates only under the condition that all countries follow identical monetary policies. These policies, however, are most likely to diverge. For instance, the rate of inflation may be higher in France than in Germany, in Italy than in the United States. If we hold on to the assumption that exchange rates between currencies remain permanently fixed, we can see that problems must develop. As wages and prices rise faster in France than in Germany, France's exports will fall and her imports will tend to rise, as long as the exchange ratio between franc and mark stays fixed. France's importers will develop a growing demand for relatively cheaper German commodities and, accordingly, for marks; and French exporters will not be able to sell as much as before to Germany (owing to relatively inflated French prices) and, accordingly, will have fewer marks to sell. At fixed exchange rates, the international-payments situation must eventually become untenable, since there will be a growing oversupply of francs and a growing shortage of marks in the foreign-exchange markets of both countries.

If price movements were permitted, such a market situation would tend to adjust itself automatically through the pressure of competition. French importers, in their eagerness to get German money, would be willing to pay more for it in terms of French money. Similarly, German exporters with an oversupply of French money on their hands would be equally willing to part with it at a lower rate in terms of German money. If these price movements were permitted, a depreciation of the franc and an appreciation of the mark would tend to reestablish the balance between exports and imports that had been destroyed by the higher rate of inflation in France. The lower price of francs in terms of marks would compensate for the relatively higher prices of commodities in France and, vice versa, French buyers would find the relatively low prices of German products less attractive once the entrance ticket to German markets, the mark, had risen in price.

What will happen if the two countries in our example keep insisting that the franc-mark ratio stay firmly fixed? How can they get out of the

1

dilemma created by combining convertibility of the currencies at fixed par values with diverging national economic policies?

An undesirable way out of this situation is that France, the deficit country in our example, would restrict imports artificially through trade or payments controls. In order to maintain fixed exchange rates, she would abolish the basic principle of convertibility. The government would decide arbitrarily who can or cannot buy German products or German money.

If trade controls and exchange restrictions are strictly ruled out, that is, if currency convertibility is maintained, and if, simultaneously, the domestic monetary policies of different countries are diverging, the exchange rates of their currencies can still be kept fixed, as long as the countries in question possess adequate international liquidity reserves that they can tap when an international payments deficit develops. In our example, the French Central Bank, the Banque de France, may be holding reserves consisting of marks, dollars, gold, or anything else that is convertible into marks. The Banque de France, then, can start selling marks as soon as the private demand for marks exceeds the private supply on the French foreign-exchange market. The exchange rate between franc and mark would remain stable, but the international liquidity reserve of France would decrease. France could also try to borrow additional reserves from various foreign sources, in particular from the German Central Bank, the Deutsche Bundesbank, or from the International Monetary Fund. But such borrowings would constitute only a temporary solution, a delay in coming to grips with the basic problem that has not yet been tackled, namely, the diverging rates of inflation of France and Germany.

A real solution could be found in the form of a speedy integration of French and German monetary policies; and what is true for these two countries would have to be true for all members of a payments system with fixed exchange rates and currency convertibility.

Through most of the recent history of international payments, the necessary integration of national monetary policies was supposed to be the more or less automatic result of changes in the international liquidity reserves of the member countries of the system. A deficit country, that is, a country that lost reserves in its effort to maintain a fixed exchange rate, was supposed to follow an anti-inflation monetary policy; a surplus country, that is, a country whose central bank had to buy foreign currencies to prevent an appreciation of its own monetary unit, was supposed to embark on a policy of domestic monetary expansion.

For many years, the ideal solution seemed to be the international gold standard. All member countries expressed the values or "parities" of their currencies in weights of gold, maintained gold convertibility, held gold reserves, and made the quantity of domestic money dependent on the size of these gold reserves. If, then, a country's rate of inflation exceeded the average rate of inflation in other countries, a deficit in international payments would appear and gold would be used to pay for the import surplus. Falling gold reserves would lead to a contraction of the domestic monetary circulation, under rules according to which a certain percentage of the monetary circulation had to be "backed" by gold. A monetary contraction in the deficit country would tend to check inflation or even lead to falling prices and wages (deflation). The country, in other words, would return to the average monetary behavior of other countries, and equilibrium in external payments would be reestablished.

The beauty of the international gold standard was, supposedly, that it automatically integrated the monetary policies of the participating countries, provided only that the latter followed certain simple rules of the game. These rules demanded that the monetary authorities of the members should contract and expand the domestic monetary circulation in response to changes in their gold reserves. Each central bank had the obligation to maintain a fixed price of gold (gold parity) and defend the national currency's convertibility into gold and, via gold, into all other gold-standard currencies. For this purpose it was imperative to make sure that the gold reserves were adequate.

Central bankers liked this game plan. It was simple and required the pursuit of anti-inflation policies, however unpopular they might be in the eyes of spendthrift government authorities.

The rules of the gold-standard game rested on the assumption that the value or purchasing power of money is determined by the quantity of money in circulation. If we increase the monetary circulation without simultaneously increasing the supply of commodities and services, prices must rise and the purchasing power of money fall. It is of paramount importance, therefore, that the quantity of money should somehow be limited.

It was logical, then, to tie the circulation of money to gold reserves that would tend to fall when an abnormally high rate of inflation produced a payments deficit and lowered the gold reserves. Fixed gold parities, therefore, enforced the needed monetary discipline.

The connection between fixed gold parities and monetary discipline explains why this one case of price-fixing found practically unanimous support—in spite of the fact that it constitutes, strictly speaking, a case of artificial price-setting, and violates the basic principle on which our market economy rests, namely, that economic decisions should be governed by price variations in preference to government interference and command.

Increasingly, the fixing of parities or exchange rates has come under attack. Economists have argued for some time that the fixing of parities is basically just as wrong as any other case of price-fixing, and that gaps between demand and supply should be automatically corrected by price changes. Deficits and surpluses in international payments would not occur if exchange rates were permitted to fluctuate freely so that they would instantly compensate for different rates of inflation in the trading countries.

The argument against fixed exchange rates (or fixed parities) grew in strength when it became increasingly obvious that the monetary authorities could no longer follow the rules of the gold standard, if playing by these rules meant the creation of mass unemployment in deficit countries. Since the world economic crisis of the early thirties, the problem of employment was considered more important than the problem of monetary stability. Up until then, employment policies were hardly known and wages and prices were still adjustable downward. As wages and prices have become increasingly rigid, a contractionist monetary policy is more likely to lead to unemployment than to falling wages and prices; and if growing unemployment is, politically speaking, even less acceptable than growing price inflation, the old discipline argument for fixed parities becomes increasingly difficult to defend.

In this situation only two choices are left. We can give up either convertibility or the fixity of exchange rates.

The introduction of exchange control, as a means for maintaining fixed parities, is basically wrong for market economies whose functioning rests on price reactions to changing market conditions. The answer would be different for Soviet-type economies, which are guided by government command rather than by a price mechanism. For the free world we must assume that it should not try to maintain fixed parities by the entirely unsuited policy of using increasingly stringent controls of international economic transactions. Currency convertibility is basically not negotiable.

Currency convertibility means that national currencies can be bought and sold freely; it does not mean that they can always be bought and sold freely *at a fixed price*. We can call convertibility at changing exchange rates *market convertibility*. It means that everybody can buy or sell a currency in any desired amount at the prevailing market price. This freedom means potential access to all raw materials, commodities, and services throughout the free world; it means *multilateralism*. Multilateralism is a situation in which a resident of country A can export his merchandise to country B and use the earned B-money to buy the currencies and products of countries C to Z. Multilateralism is essential for vigorous international trade, but it does not require fixed exchange rates.

If it is impossible to achieve integration of the monetary policies of the members of the international payments system, and if payments controls are to be avoided, there is a perfectly acceptable alternative left. The exchange rates must be permitted to behave as the prices they really are.

A system without fixed parities need not take the form of freely fluctuating exchange rates, that is, rates exclusively determined by the play of private market forces. The monetary authorities can continue to *influence* the exchange rates through selling and buying operations; they can *intervene* in the foreign-exchange markets to the extent that they are willing to let their international liquidity reserves decrease or increase.

Between the old gold standard, in which the monetary authorities promised to maintain *permanently* fixed parities, and a system with *freely* fluctuating exchange rates, in which the authorities do not interfere at all, lies a continuum of unlimited possibilities, from very rare and major adjustments of parities to a mere smoothing of daily fluctuations by the monetary authorities.

If a country's rate of inflation is higher than that of its trading partners, if its international liquidity reserves are low, and if anti-inflation measures would produce a sharp decrease in the rate of employment, the country could be permitted to devalue its currency vis-à-vis a common denominator, such as gold or the U.S. dollar. This devaluation would increase the country's exports and decrease its imports. Similarly, a country with a low rate of inflation and an increasing surplus in its external balance could upvalue its currency, that is, make it more expensive for foreigners and thereby correct the balance.

An upvaluation, however, is, as a rule, less urgent than a devaluation, and this is why upvaluations happen much more rarely than devaluations. When a deficit country runs out of reserves it can no longer intervene in the foreign exchange market by selling foreign exchange or gold; it then has to devalue if it wants to maintain the market convertibility of its currency. When the central bank of a surplus country buys currencies of deficit countries with the intention of avoiding an appreciation of its own monetary unit, liquidity reserves increase and nothing has to be done about it. Growing liquidity reserves are an indication that a country's money is undervalued, that is, that it would have appreciated under free market conditions. From the standpoint of the country's export industry, undervaluation is a pleasant state of affairs. It gives an artificial competitive advantage to the country, and the accumulation of liquidity reserves is viewed as a proud sign of the country's economic strength and disciplined monetary policy.

However, even surplus countries may eventually find it advisable to adjust their parities. A surplus country can maintain a fixed par value only if its central bank purchases all the foreign money that its exporters cannot sell at the fixed parity. These purchases are made with newly issued domestic money and increase the domestic monetary circulation, while the export surplus reduces the commodities that are for sale in the domestic markets. More money chases fewer goods. The resulting price inflation can become so severe that it may eventually create the political climate in which an upvaluation will be undertaken, even against violent protests of the export industry.

A system with relatively more devaluations than upvaluations is, obviously, unsymmetrical. The deficit countries have to devalue unless they can borrow additional liquidity reserves or use exchange restrictions; the surplus countries, on the other hand, enjoy the competitive undervaluation of their currencies until inflation forces them into belated action.

Another shortcoming of a system with rare but substantial parity changes is the fact that it is crisis-prone. The difficulties of the deficit countries become highly visible and advertise coming devaluations. Since parities are no longer permanently fixed but can be adjusted in cases of so-called fundamental disequilibria (such as too high a rate of inflation or of unemployment), it is easy for private speculators to anticipate parity changes and to make their own anticipations self-fulfilling through the selling of currencies of deficit and the buying of currencies of surplus countries.

A regime of rare parity changes in cases of "fundamental" disequilibria was introduced in Bretton Woods, N.H., at the end of World War II. The Bretton Woods system was a compromise of two opposed tendencies: on the one hand, the desire to safeguard the benefits to be derived from fixed parities, and on the other, the urgent demand for greater leeway in domestic employment policies. Together with currency convertibility, this combination made for an unstable system. To put it differently, the Bretton Woods Agreement tried to hold on to the practices of the gold standard while the abolition of permanently fixed par values eliminated the discipline that had been the core of the old system.

The Bretton Woods Conference of 1944 established the International Monetary Fund, which was to give "confidence to members by making the Fund's resources available to them under adequate safeguards, thus providing them with the opportunity to correct maladjustments in their balance of payments without resorting to measures destructive of national and international prosperity." Such destructive policies had been followed during the interwar period, in the form of competitive exchange depreciation, of domestic deflation with the result of mass unemployment, and of introducing stifling exchange and trade restrictions.

The Fund was to end these practices: first, by making additional liquidity reserves available; second, by exerting pressure toward greater integration of national monetary policies; and third, by permitting adjustments of parities in rare cases. But for many years this third possibility was considered a measure of last resort, to be avoided at almost any cost.

The Fund's resources were very modest and its power to exert pressure on members in payments surplus was practically nil, since these countries did not need the help of the Fund. That the Bretton Woods system made a good start in spite of these weaknesses was due to the fact that the United States was willing to finance the then existing payments deficits in the free world. In the process, the U.S. dollar became the world's "key currency." The world was, for all practical purposes, on a dollar standard.

When, by about 1958, the reconstruction era had come to an end, the economies of Europe and Japan became, once more, serious competitors for the United States. To be sure, most other countries still suffered from a dollar shortage, but aid dollars for less-developed countries were no longer very welcome when they found their way into the central banks of Germany, France, or Japan, via the multilateral payments system. For these countries, the dollar shortage had gradually changed into a dollar glut; but they had to keep on buying dollars to prevent an appreciation of their currencies vis-à-vis the dollar. The dollar had taken on the role of international money. It was supposedly gold-convertible and served not only as international numéraire, but also as intervention currency when central banks tried to maintain fixed parities.

As the dollar glut developed, this situation became disquieting. Hitherto the system had rested on the belief that the dollar would remain permanently fixed in terms of gold. However, growing dollar balances in the rest of the world, together with shrinking gold reserves in the United States, suggested that the time would have to come when the dollar would have to be devalued by raising the dollar price of gold. An ever-growing payments deficit of the United States suggested that the dollar had become overvalued in terms of currencies that, only a few years before, the United States had helped to support.

The overvaluation of the dollar had two reasons. One was the decreasing competitiveness of the U.S. economy in consequence of the reconstruction of the economies of Europe and Japan; the other was the fact that the U.S. dollar, as key currency, was tied to gold, so that the safety valve of devaluation did not apply to the United States.

The countries with the growing dollar glut argued that the United States was making unfair use of the fact that she could finance her payments deficits by "automatic borrowing," knowing that the surplus countries had to buy and hold dollars whenever they wanted to prevent an appreciation of their own currencies vis-à-vis the dollar. The United States, on the other hand, was arguing that, far from enjoying an unfair advantage, her economy was laboring under the handicap of an overvalued parity.

When the United States announced on August 15, 1971 the suspension of dollar convertibility into gold (the closing of the "gold window"), a breakdown of the international monetary system did not occur, but neither did the measure solve the international monetary problem. Even after a dollar devaluation and a general realignment of parities at the end of 1971, the basic problem was still the same as before—the incompatibility of the desire to maintain stable par values with the failure to integrate the monetary policy of the members of the system; and the difficulty to adjust the supply of international liquidity reserves to this situation, while simultaneously releasing the dollar from its role as key currency.

As the basic weaknesses of the system found expression in repeated payments crises, interesting suggestions were made as to how the system could benefit from more frequent changes in par values. These proposals, however, did not prevail against the strong preference of practitioners and government officials for fixed par values. Finally, in 1973, the par-value system broke down. One after another, the leading nations permitted their currencies to "float," that is, permitted the foreign-exchange markets to behave like real markets, with price variations whenever needed to balance demand and supply.

The first impression was that the Bretton Woods regime had come to an end in the sense that fixed parities were now supplanted by freely fluctuating exchange rates. Suddenly we seemed to have gone from one extreme to the other. It soon became clear, however, that the Central Banks of the member countries were not willing to remain inactive in the foreign-exchange markets, to let private speculation reign unchecked, and to stand idly by should other countries try to practice competitive depreciation. In short, the floating of the exchange rates was managed and not free.

Under the given circumstances, the system of managed floating worked far better than the system with fixed but adjustable par values. Major international monetary crises stopped occurring; as a matter of fact, the new regime proved to be so shock-resistant that even the international oil crisis did not provoke a new upheaval in international payments.

It would be an exaggeration to say that the Bretton Woods regime has broken down: first, because changes in parities were permitted and could have been used more frequently, so that it can be argued that the operation and not the structure of the system was at fault; and second, because all along the spirit of cooperation prevailed. These facts suggest that a reconstruction of the system, mainly on the basis of more flexible exchange rates, is possible.

The following pages make the attempt to tell the story of international money in simple language; to show how international payments worked under the gold standard before 1914, and why chaotic conditions developed during the interwar period; how the International Monetary Fund was created, and why its weaknesses led to the emergence of a dollar standard; and how the insistence on combining inconsistent elements had to lead to managed floating. Finally, the book will try to explain how greater flexibility of exchange rates can give the international monetary system greater elasticity and coherence.

2

Gold and Gold-Exchange Standard

The Gold Mechanism

The international gold standard of the days before World War I is the prototype of a consistent international payments mechanism. Historical as well as theoretical reasons suggest that it be studied first. Today's international monetary arrangements are still influenced by gold, and some experts even recommend the return to a modernized version of the gold standard as a remedy for most of our monetary ills.

The international gold standard rested on the following assumptions. The currencies of the member countries were backed by gold reserves, and the monetary authorities (central banks and treasuries) stood ready to buy and sell gold in unlimited amounts at a permanently fixed price, the so-called gold parity. Gold was the international unit of account and established the exchange rates between the member currencies. It was their common anchorage.

Assume now that under these conditions a country's imports (of commodities, services, and securities) exceed its exports as to their total value. Since exports earn foreign exchange and imports have to be paid in foreign exchange, importers want to buy more foreign money than exporters have to sell. This situation tends to raise the price of foreign money in terms of local money, owing to competitive bidding by the market parties. In other words, the deficit country's currency tends to depreciate and the surplus country's to appreciate. These exchange-rate variations, however, can be only very limited under gold-standard conditions. They cannot exceed the upper or lower gold point. Buyers of foreign exchange, for example, would not be willing to pay a price higher than the upper gold point, because at that price they could procure foreign exchange through the shipment of gold, since they can always buy gold at the fixed price at home, send it abroad, and sell it there at the fixed price. Similarly, sellers of foreign exchange (which they earned through exports) would not accept a price lower than the gold-import point, at which it would always be possible to cash in claims on foreign money via gold imports.

The spread between the gold points indicated the extent to which the exchange rates of gold-standard currencies could fluctuate—like a snake in

9

a tunnel. The "band" within which variations were permitted was equal to twice the transfer cost of gold, that is, the cost of shipment, insurance, and loss of interest during the transaction.

Variations of exchange rates between the gold points exerted an equilibrating influence on international payments, by stimulating a deficit country's exports through a slight depreciation of its currency and by toning down its imports. More important, however, was the fact that these small fluctuations of a country's exchange rate tended to stimulate equilibrating capital movements. Depreciation of a deficit country's currency induced foreign capitalists to buy it in the firm expectation of a rebound, that is, a return to its gold parity, at which it could then be sold at a profit.

These equilibrating capital movements were important for the smooth functioning of the gold mechanism. The flow of capital from surplus to deficit countries provided time for the needed monetary adjustment, that is, for a contraction of the monetary circulation of the country.

As a rule, gold did not really flow between deficit and surplus countries, provided that the deficit countries were alert and defended their gold reserves by appropriate policies. The latter amounted, in the main, to the raising of the rate of interest to reduce the demand for credit until inflation was halted and the prices of export commodities became more competitive. While the effect of higher rates of interest on commodity prices was slow, their effect on the inflow of foreign capital was swift. Higher rates of interest combined with the temporary depreciation of the currency to make equilibrating flows of capital attractive and to help a deficit country in its smooth return to external balance.

We see that the international gold standard combined permanently fixed gold parities with a narrow band for exchange-rate variations. As a matter of fact, central bankers sometimes tried to push the gold points apart to gain more flexibility. This could easily be done by raising the bank's selling price over the buying price of gold.

Equilibrating capital movements, however, did not cure the basic cause of the difficulty, the higher rate of inflation in the deficit country. In the long run, the country had to reduce its monetary circulation, while a country with deflation was supposed to expand it until balance between exports and imports was reestablished.

While the national monetary systems of the gold-standard countries differed in technical detail, they had this in common: the creation or contraction of the monetary circulation was connected with the countries' official gold reserves through gold-backing requirements. If there were no extra or "buffer" reserves available, an outflow of gold led to a contraction of the country's monetary circulation equal to a certain multiple of the loss of gold reserves. This contraction had the deflationary effect of lowering wages and prices, of increasing exports, and of decreasing imports. If commodity prices rose in all countries, it was sufficient if a gold outflow reduced the deficit country's rate of inflation to the average level.

Surplus countries with a gold inflow were supposed to expand their monetary circulation on the basis of their growing gold reserve. Other things remaining equal, prices and wages would rise, imports would increase, and exports fall. The gold mechanism was supposed to work symmetrically. Eventually, the gold would flow back from where it had come, reestablishing an even distribution of gold reserves among the gold-standard countries.

Advantages and Shortcomings of the Gold Mechanism

The international gold mechanism is said to have had the following advantages.

First, it maintained permanently fixed parities between the member currencies, yet permitted, between the gold points, slight variations of exchange rates. Fixed parities served as reliable and stable foundation for international transactions, while minor variations of exchange rates gave the system flexibility through an equilibrating flow of short-term capital. Movements of gold from country to country were the exception rather than the rule.

Second, the gold mechanism forced the monetary authorities to integrate their policies with those of other gold-standard countries. Countries with inflation had to contract, countries with deflation to expand their monetary circulation. Prolonged divergencies in monetary policy were made impossible. If the members played the game according to its rules, their reactions were automatic. A supervising international authority was thought unnecessary. Central bankers were satisfied with the rules of the game, which gave them clear-cut directions and enabled them to refute their governments' request that they should finance budget deficits through money creation. In other words, the gold mechanism acted as disciplinarian.

Third, the gold mechanism provided for equilibrating capital movements, not only because of the already mentioned minor fluctuations in exchange rates, but also because the monetary authorities in the deficit and surplus countries used changes in interest rates to operate the mechanism. A deficit country had to raise, a surplus country to lower the cost of borrowing, thereby inducing private capital to flow from surplus to deficit countries and to provide needed liquidity reserves for the latter. The equilibrating flow of capital toned down the harshness of the gold mechanism as disciplinarian. If the system did lead to deflation and depression in deficit countries, it was argued that further delay would have made the consequences of monetary contraction even less attractive.

These were the advantages commonly ascribed to the payments regime that connected the major trading countries before World War I. Closer scrutiny, however, reveals serious shortcomings of the gold mechanism even during its heyday. It did not achieve worldwide monetary stability, and suffered from a built-in bias toward deflation.

Gold-losing deficit countries had to contract their monetary circulation, even if this contraction was felt to be undesirable because it lowered the national income and created unemployment. That governments were at all willing to follow deflationary policies (which are practically unthinkable today) can be explained by the virtual absence of conscious employment policies before World War I.

Monetary expansion in response to an inflow of gold reserves was much less certain than a contraction in the opposite case. Interest rates might be lowered in surplus countries according to the rules of the game, but low rates did not always call forth increased investment and growing monetary circulation when low profit expectations compared unfavorably even with low rates of interest. However, if surplus countries with growing gold reserves were unable to increase their monetary circulation, the gold-losing deficit countries had to shoulder the adjustment burden one-sidedly. When surplus countries were unable to inflate, the deficit countries had to deflate even more. In other words, the gold mechanism did not work symmetrically.

When the deficit countries' deflation policies created depression and unemployment, the external adjustment worked via falling imports rather than via growing exports, and in the end, even the surplus countries had to suffer. Falling income and employment in the deficit countries was transmitted to the economies of the surplus countries through a falling volume of world trade.

The international gold standard was not deflation and depression proof; but neither was it sure to prevent worldwide inflation. The layman often believes that gold imparts intrinsic and unchanging value to the currencies it backs. Nothing could be further from the truth. The monetary value of gold is the product of national policies, which can be quite inflationary. The value of money depends on its power to purchase commodities, and this purchasing power is determined by the prices of the goods it buys. Prices, in turn, depend on the quantity of money and the frequency of its turnover —the so-called velocity of circulation of money—in relation to the supply of commodities and services in the markets of the economy. Even before 1914, the quantity of money was only very loosely connected with a country's gold reserve. Depending on legal or customary reserve requirements, a change in the gold reserve could lead to a ten- or twentyfold expansion or contraction of the domestic monetary circulation, provided that the game was played according to its rules, that is, without the attempt on the part of the members to accumulate buffer reserves.

The backing requirements, which differed substantially from country to country, changed over the years, but always in the direction of growing permissiveness and liberalization, particularly in connection with the growing use of bank money (demand deposits). It is important to understand that as long as all gold-standard countries liberalized their backing requirements in unison and produced the same rate of inflation, the gold standard could not prevent world prices from rising. It could only slow individual members of the system down to an average rate of inflation.

Advocates of the gold standard answer that worldwide inflation would soon be stopped under gold-standard conditions. Fixed gold parities would make gold mining unprofitable if all commodity prices (with the exception of the gold price) were increasing. Gold reserves would then grow more slowly and world inflation would end. However, this process would be glacially slow, while, in the meantime, its effect on the quantity of money could easily be overcompensated by the above-mentioned liberalization of gold-backing requirements.

We can see that the gold standard could prevent neither depression nor inflation. Asymmetry in its working promoted depression while continued liberalization of backing requirements opened the door to worldwide credit creation. It may seem as if the gold standard could not simultaneously be blamed for inflationary and deflationary effects, or that both tendencies would have to cancel one another. The argument is not contradictory, however. The deflationary effect of a loss of gold reserves could be very hard on a deficit country if the surplus countries were unable or unwilling to expand. This asymmetry was caused by the fact that a central bank can technically always bring about a credit contraction, but not an expansion, since it cannot force private banks and their customers to borrow. For purposes of monetary expansion a surplus country may need the aid of government deficit spending, which was taboo under gold-standard rules. The danger of worldwide inflation, on the other hand, was caused by the fact that the system lacked supranational leadership by an international institution. Nobody tried to formulate common gold-backing requirements. The international gold standard was an orchestra without conductor.

Occasionally, the inflation resulting from a general liberalization of backing requirements had the positive effect of toning down the deflationary pressures resulting from the system's asymmetry. Alvin H. Hansen suggests that the functioning of the pre-1914 gold standard was "greatly facilitated by the circumstance that it operated in a rapidly growing economy and under the favorable condition of an upward trend in prices." [1] Another factor that supported the functioning of the gold standard was Great Britain's dominant role in world finance. Through short-term capital flows she gave greater flexibility to a basically rigid arrangement.

On the whole, the gold standard did not work badly; but neither did it correspond to the textbook picture of an automatic adjustment mechanism. It maintained fixed parities and external balance, but only because international-payments equilibrium was given unquestioned priority over a high employment level. If the gold standard looks, in retrospect, perhaps somewhat better than it was, it derives its luster from being compared with the international monetary chaos that prevailed during the interwar period.

The Gold-Exchange Standard

After World War I it was taken for granted that the world would return to the gold standard. However, war inflation had reduced gold production, and the world's gold was very unequally distributed as a result of the war. How was the gold standard to be reestablished under these conditions? Would not a general scramble for gold lead to worldwide deflation, as the different countries tried to outcompete each other in their eagerness to regain adequate gold reserves?

The problem was solved by the adoption of a makeshift gold standard, the so-called gold-exchange standard, in which a shortage of gold reserves is overcome by the device of maintaining additional international liquidity reserves in the form of gold-convertible currencies. Even before 1914 a few countries had held their reserves in foreign exchange; the gold-exchange standard was not revolutionary.

The Genoa Conference of 1922 recommended adoption of the gold-exchange standard. Some countries would remain on the gold standard and maintain gold-convertibility of their currencies, while others would hold their international liquidity reserves mainly in the "hard" currencies of the former. As before, changes in international reserves would induce the members of the system to integrate their monetary policies to achieve external balance. The Genoa Conference did not create an international monetary institution, but the new standard put the countries with gold-convertible currencies into a strategic position. The supply of international liquidity was now largely determined by the policies of the hard-currency countries. We shall see that they did not live up to their implied responsibilities.

The gold-exchange standard was even less symmetrical than the gold standard. When hard-currency reserves rather than gold flowed in response to trade deficits, a hard-currency country in surplus received its own currency rather than gold, and was even less likely thereupon to expand its monetary circulation. Even more than before, the adjustment burden had to be shouldered by the deficit countries for which a loss of gold-convertible currencies, say francs or dollars, was fully as serious as a loss of gold previously.

The poorer countries had to borrow hard currencies or to earn them via export surpluses. To achieve the latter, the temptation was great to undervalue their currencies for competitive reasons. There was no international authority to police the system and to see to it that realistic parities were adopted and maintained.

When new parities were chosen after World War I, they were adopted on a hit-or-miss basis. Monetary authorities still believed that national price levels could be adjusted to wrongly chosen parities. However, this was true only for *under*valuations, which implied a competitive advantage vis-à-vis other countries. *Over*valuations, which had to be counterbalanced by domestic price deflation, proved extremely damaging. As experience was gained, more and more countries tried to err in the direction of undervaluation or competitive exchange depreciation.

Out of these difficulties grew John Maynard Keynes's insistence that a currency's external value (that is, its parity) should be altered frequently so as to conform to whatever real internal value or purchasing power results from domestic policies.[2]

We meet here with a fundamental shift of emphasis away from the fixed-parities doctrine of the gold standard. Domestic full-employment policies tended to become the primary aim of national economic policy, and to push external balance at fixed parities into second place. As this tendency grew during the interwar period, it became less and less likely that the members of the system could be made to play according to the rules of the gold-standard game. Fixed parities could be combined with convertibility when currencies were undervalued—overvalued parities, however, could only be maintained when convertibility was abolished, that is, when exchange restrictions were introduced.

Undervaluation, competitive exchange depreciation, and exchange controls are so-called beggar-my-neighbor policies. They try to increase the domestic employment level at the expense of other countries. In the end, however, beggar-my-neighbor policies invariably backfire. Gains in domestic employment at the expense of growing unemployment in other countries will not last. They lead

to consequences of which the most hardbitten nationalist must take account. For other countries, finding themselves in a more wretched plight than ever, will have strong motives for protecting themselves, by tariffs, devaluation, or wage cuts. Retaliation will begin, and before long all nations of the world will be playing a frantic game of beggar-my-neighbor . . . [and] considered collectively, all are worse off than before.[3]

All this is now undisputed, particularly since we have at our disposal employment policies that do not rest on unfair advantages taken in the international trade and payments field.

The Interwar Period

The international-payments picture of the interwar years is very complex. However, examples taken from four major countries can give a general idea of the gradual deterioration of the situation.

Different rates of inflation in the various countries during and after World War I should have led to a general realignment of parities on realistic levels before the gold-exchange standard started to operate. Since prices in Great Britain had risen by about 10 percent more than prices in the United States, the pound sterling, for instance, should not have been fixed at its prewar dollar parity. The new rate should have been adjusted to changes in the purchasing-power parity of pound and dollar, that is, their changed ability to purchase commodities at inflated domestic prices. Though prices had risen more in England than in the United States, normal trade relations could have been resumed had the pound been devalued correspondingly. Unfortunately, the Chancellor of the Exchequer, Winston Churchill, insisted on maintaining the prewar dollar parity of the pound sterling, and thereby unnecessarily put the British economy into a most precarious position. The enormous difficulties of bringing about a general reduction of prices and wages were, according to John Maynard Keynes, misunderstood and underrated.[4] The attempt to correct the effects of overvaluation through domestic deflation led to the disastrous coal strike of 1926. The British wage and price structure had become too rigid. The effort to lower it brought depression and stagnation.

The depreciation of the pound sterling in 1931 reversed the external position of the British economy. Since England's depreciation was not followed for several years by the United States and the gold-bloc countries of Europe, England now enjoyed an artificial competitive advantage and "achieved the best of two worlds: (1) an export advantage over competitors, and (2) an improvement of trade through exchange stability with countries complementary to her economy,"[5] which had tied their currencies to the pound rather than to gold because they were England's main suppliers of raw materials. These were the so-called sterling-club countries. Since the gold-bloc members refused to follow the British depreciation, they subjected their economies to the same difficulties from which England had just emerged. The British depreciation thus became in fact, though perhaps not in intention, a competitive depreciation and, in 1932, after a renewed fixing of the gold parity, a competitive undervaluation.

The sterling club constituted a pure exchange standard, a standard without reference to gold (other than the gold parity of the pound). Countries with close political, commercial, and financial ties with the United Kingdom pegged their currencies to the pound rather than gold. Their reserves consisted of pound-sterling balances in London banks. The United

Kingdom, the center of the bloc, could, of course, not "go off sterling." If, therefore, members of the bloc devalued, the United Kingdom might suffer a competitive disadvantage. On the other hand, London had the benefit of an inflow of short-term funds if bloc members insisted on preventing an appreciation of their currencies through official purchases of pound sterling. These developments foreshadowed today's dollar problem.

Price inflation in France had been so bad during and after World War I that it was out of the question to maintain the prewar dollar parity, that is, follow the mistake Churchill made. The franc was permitted to depreciate. In 1926, France returned to gold, but the chosen parity constituted a decisive undervaluation of the franc, which produced export surpluses and forced the Banque de France into continued purchases of gold and foreign currencies in an effort to prevent an appreciation of the franc. This tendency was aggravated by a repatriation of French capital that had left the country before the return to gold.

In 1928, it was decided that the Banque de France should no longer buy foreign currencies. This meant that deficits of other countries with France had to lead to a flow of gold into France. France thus violated the rules of the gold-exchange standard, which had been created expressly to avoid excessive deflationary pressures on deficit countries.

The British depreciation and the formation of the sterling bloc in 1931 reversed France's competitive position. The strange fact that the formerly undervalued French parity was maintained, even when it constituted a substantial overvaluation, must be explained by the fear of renewed domestic inflation under the impact of a devaluation. Rising import prices, it was thought, would lead to new rounds of wage and price increases. Despite England's sad experiences between 1925 and 1931, the French authorities obviously still believed in the practicability of a deflation. In the end, however, France, too, had to learn that credit contraction reduced employment rather than wages and prices. Unwilling to devalue, and reluctant to deflate, France could not balance her external accounts, and turned to the use of import quotas. In other words, in maintaining her overvalued parity, France was forced to give up multilateralism. Finally, France and the few remaining gold-bloc countries of Western Europe had to follow the British and American devaluations. The cycle of depreciations and devaluations had run its full course by 1936.

The economy of the United States was exposed to a major deflation from 1920 to 1921. From 1922 to 1929 prices remained stable and the impression was created that we had finally learned to combine monetary stability with full employment. Major technical advances in industry and agriculture led to falling costs of production. However, a vastly growing social product could not be sold at stable prices without an increase in monetary circulation. This was the period of hidden inflation in which low rates of interest, combined with high profit expectations, led to overinvestment. However, once all productive resources were fully employed, further money creation had to slow down to avoid price inflation. At rising rates of interest (and with falling profit expectations) the investment boom collapsed. The severe economic crisis that followed was aggravated and prolonged by a banking system whose rigid backing requirements prevented the monetary authorities from creating adequate domestic liquidity.

The falling-off of U.S. imports under the impact of the crisis of 1929 and the following economic stagnation constitutes the classic case of a transmission of economic difficulties from country to country through the medium of international payments. The supply of dollars to other countries via purchases of their commodities, services, and securities decreased by 68 percent between 1929 and 1932!

While this situation could not be quickly cured by the domestic economic policies that were known at the time, its international effects could have been cushioned through increased foreign lending. Instead, foreign U.S. credits were curtailed and outstanding short-term loans recalled, to the detriment of the countries that had relied on the facilities of the gold-exchange standard.

To repay their foreign borrowings, the deficit countries had to try to achieve export surpluses through contractionist domestic policies, which aggravated the impact of the U.S. depression on their economies. Furthermore, the very efforts of the debtors to repay in terms of goods and services was met by the raising of the U.S. tariff wall to the highest level in the history of the country. This policy revealed even more glaringly than the untimely withdrawal of short-term loans an astonishing inconsistency in the foreign economic behavior of a major credit country.

Finally, in 1933 to 1934, the gold parity of the dollar was changed from $20.67 to $35.00 per ounce, a substantial *devaluation* of the currency of a *surplus* country! It is hard to find plausible reasons for this culminating inconsistency. Probably it was in the main an attempt to raise the domestic price level via increasing the prices of imported commodities. This anti-deflation policy did not succeed. The dollar devaluation increased the dollar value of U.S. gold reserves. Again it could be seen, however, that increasing liquidity alone does not increase investment and employment.

A sketch of the highlights of the international monetary situation between the wars would be incomplete without a glance at the very special German case. Germany's postwar inflation had raised prices by one *trillion* times before the mark was stabilized in November 1923 and Germany could start to rebuild her economy. However, Germany was still faced with the problem of having to pay reparations by achieving a large excess of exports over imports as the only way in which a *real* transfer of unilateral payments can take place. For several years the problem was evaded by the simple device of borrowing privately more than had officially to be paid as reparation. About half of the money that flowed into Germany as foreign credit was handed back as reparation payment, thus transforming a political into a private debt. This practice was particularly dangerous since about one-half of the private foreign loans were of a short-term nature and could be called back at a moment's notice.

When foreign capital stopped flowing into Germany and the banking crisis in the United States led to a frantic attempt to liquidate foreign loans, the precarious nature of the whole scenario became evident. The so-called transfer problem became real. Germany had to develop an enormous export surplus if she wanted to pay her private foreign creditors and possibly also reparations. An export surplus could be achieved through devaluation or deflation. Inordinate fear of domestic price inflation, owing to the experiences of 1923, made it seem unwise to follow a devaluation policy. Germany decided on deflation; and since a purely monetary deflation through credit contraction seemed far too slow, prices, wages, and interest rates were lowered by emergency decree under the Weimar Constitution. This policy caused the rapid rise in unemployment that helped Adolf Hitler to gain power in 1933. Hitler then "solved" the international payments problem by refusing to pay reparations and by abolishing currency convertibility.

Germany's experiences are important because they teach us, first, that deflation by emergency decree is dangerous in a market economy in which it will cause mass unemployment, and second, that huge unilateral payments can create serious problems. This second experience applies even to payments such as grants-in-aid from rich to poor countries. These payments, too, have to be transferred, and this transfer problem can add substantially to the complexities of an international payments system, as the experiences of the United States after World War II have shown.

The Keynesian Revolution

Out of the Great Depression of 1929 and after grew the so-called Keynesian revolution.[6] The new economics of Keynes held that the governments of market economies have the duty to maintain adequate levels of domestic demand to ensure high levels of employment. Monetary policies alone were no longer considered capable of guaranteeing that all private savings, forthcoming at high levels of national income, can find investment outlets. Saved money is money that is not spent on consumption. If it is not spent on investment goods either, deficient total demand will cause unemployment. Then fiscal policies, mainly in the form of deficit spending, will have to be used. This fiscal policy may easily conflict with the monetary policies prescribed by gold-standard arrangements. The need for government deficit spending stems from the fact that private investment demand may not react positively to a mere lowering of interest rates by the monetary authorities.

It must not be assumed, however, that all the economic difficulties of 1929 and after were produced by this inherent weakness of the private-enterprise system. To a large extent they were caused by incompetent government interference that did not permit the markets to function properly. The long list of inconsistent policies in international economic relations during the interwar period suggests that market economies cannot be expected to work normally in such a climate.

However, modern market economies can no longer be left entirely unmanaged, because we no longer have a system with sufficiently elastic prices and wages. Since prices and wages have lost their downward adjustability, creeping inflation has become practically unavoidable where high employment levels are being maintained. When price movements work reliably only in an upward direction, the operation of the price mechanism must result in price inflation. When monetary authorities try to achieve price stability under these circumstances, they cause unemployment as long as wages tend to increase faster than productivity.

Today, these facts are generally accepted, but this unanimity leaves much room for differences of opinion concerning the choice of policies that are to lead us as close as possible to the ideal of high employment at stable prices. Such differences of opinion exist not only within but also between different countries. The members of the international payments system, therefore, should be left free to choose their own preferred blend of domestic and foreign economic policies if we want them to join an international monetary institution and to follow prescribed rules of international economic behavior. Most certainly, they are no longer willing to play according to the rules of the gold-standard game.

3 The International Monetary Fund and the Dollar

The Keynes Plan

Efforts to create a new international-payments system after World War II had two major objectives: first, to eliminate the worst features of the old system, particularly competitive exchange depreciations and exchange controls, and second, to give the members sufficient freedom in the pursuit of their domestic economic policies. Full employment and balanced growth of international trade were considered compatible, since countries with high employment levels are less inclined to beggar their neighbors.

The monetary experts who met toward the end of World War II in Bretton Woods to discuss a thorough reconstruction of the world's monetary system were in agreement that a mere return to the gold-exchange standard was not enough. They tried to find a compromise between fixed parities on the one hand and reasonable freedom for their national economic policies on the other. Fixed parities were desired as protection against competitive depreciation and disequilibrating capital movements, but they implied many of the strict features of the gold standard, and tended to interfere with freedom for domestic policies. This basic conflict could be overcome in several ways. For instance, if the members of the system could count on the availability of large international liquidity reserves, they might possibly be able to coordinate their policies without damaging deflation. But the supply of liquidity reserves would have to be far more secure and orderly than under the gold-exchange standard. The erratic behavior of the hard-currency countries would have to be replaced through the creation of a permanent international institution, whose resources would be at the disposal of needy members at all times. If members were not able to reach external balance at fixed parities and would, accordingly, have to face the choice between domestic mass unemployment and currency devaluation, the international institution could, in some rare cases, permit changes in the members' par values while still protecting the system against competitive exchange depreciation. Furthermore, exchange controls need not be suddenly and entirely abolished. While basically suspect, they would still be needed during the transition period, and possibly also to handle disequilibrating capital movements.

The Bretton Woods Conference of 1944 was preceded by discussions

21

which centered, in the main, around two proposals: the American or White Plan (after its chief author Harry D. White) and the British or Keynes Plan.[1] White suggested that all member countries of the new system should contribute certain amounts of gold and of their national currencies to a common International Stabilization Fund, whose resources would then be available to help deficit countries maintain par values in relation to gold without having to resort to exchange controls and other destructive policies. Parity adjustments were to be permitted, but "only when essential to the correction of fundamental disequilibrium" in a member's balance of payments and "only with the approval of three-fourths of the member votes." Since the resources of White's Stabilization Fund were to be made available "under conditions prescribed," we may assume that White's Fund would have tried to influence the domestic policies of the members.

Since the compromise of Bretton Woods followed, in the main, the outline of the White Plan, we can limit our preliminary discussion to the British or Keynes Plan for establishment of an International Clearing Union.

The Keynes Plan dispensed with the idea of a common reserve pool. Instead of contributing gold or national currencies, the members of the Union would have been asked to agree to accept payments by other members in the form of having international bank money, called *bancor,* credited to their accounts in the books of the Union. To put it differently, deficit countries could have paid for needed foreign currencies with *bancor* checks. The limit for such *bancor* drawings would have been determined by a country's quota. Since the debit entry for a paying country would always have been equal to the credit entry for the payee-surplus country, debits and credits would have balanced automatically in the books of the Clearing Union.

However, while the right of a deficit country to pay for foreign money with *bancor* checks was strictly limited by its quota, the duty of a surplus country to accept *bancor* payments would have been unlimited, or limited only by the aggregate of quotas of all deficit countries. This was very significant, since at the end of World War II the United States was about the only major creditor country. As most other countries were likely to develop huge deficits, the United States' obligation to accept *bancor* checks could have reached an amount close to the total of quotas of the rest of the members of the Union. This was the first reason the representatives of the United States felt it necessary to reject the Keynes Plan.

In trying to grasp the essence of the Keynes Plan it is important to remember that Keynes was eager to grant all members the right to pursue full-employment policies of their own choice. At fixed par values, this implied a massive supply of international liquidity reserves. Keynes suggested a total of quotas of about $33 billion, including a quota of $3 billion for the United States. If we make the then realistic assumption of deficit positions for most of the member countries, we can see that enormous *bancor* balances could have piled up in favor of, and with inflationary consequences for, the United States. By comparison, the obligations of the United States under the White Plan would have been limited to a quota of $2.75 billion plus the willingness to buy gold from the Stabilization Fund. With hindsight we know that Keynes's figures were far more realistic than the figures of the White Plan and of the International Monetary Fund which followed White's scheme. The original supply of international liquidity in the International Monetary Fund was limited to the paid-in gold and the currency contributions of the surplus countries, altogether perhaps not more than about one-sixth of the *bancor* supply in the Clearing Union.

Keynes did not believe that fixed par values were the core of the new system, but admitted the need for "an orderly and agreed method to determine the relative exchange values of national currency units, so that unilateral action and competitive depreciations are prevented." He proposed that the International Clearing Union should make frequent and almost automatic use of parity adjustments, by insisting on "a stated reduction in the value of a member's currency" when a member's deficit in the Union were rising. Also, surplus countries were supposed to upvalue their currencies when their credit balance with the Union exceeded one-half of their quota. Since the United States' credit balance would soon have climbed to many times the U.S. quota, the dollar would have been in for frequent upvaluations—a second reason for United States' representatives to reject the Keynes Plan.

Keynes was conscious of the fact that the gold-exchange standard had worked asymmetrically. The adjustment burden had rested one-sidedly on the deficit countries which, in defending their international liquidity reserves, had been forced to deflate their economies, while the surplus countries had been under no compulsion to inflate. Keynes felt that it was of paramount importance to emphasize the responsibility of the surplus countries, a fact that was already revealed in the request that they be obliged to extend credit in the form of *bancor* not up to the limit of their own quotas but possibly close to the quotas of all deficit countries together. Continuous upvaluation of surplus currencies was seen as a major equilibrating device. Fascinating, too, was Keynes's suggestion that interest charges should be paid on both debit *and credit* balances in the Union as "a significant indication that the system looks on excessive credit balances with as critical an eye as on excessive debit balances."

As already reported, Keynes's proposals were rejected by the U.S. experts, who dreaded to accept for the United States the responsibilities of a lonely surplus or creditor country in the framework of the Clearing Union. However, in the end the United States made more dollars available *outside* the International Monetary Fund than would have been needed to finance her obligations under the Keynes Plan. This point is of great importance. The inadequacy of the resources of the Fund pushed the dollar into its key-currency role, and produced thereby many of the problems that plague us today. Keynes, having watched the malfunctioning of the gold-exchange standard, wanted to prevent the repetition of a situation in which the world's monetary system would depend too one-sidedly on the fortunes of major national currencies. The members of the Clearing Union would have been expected "to keep their reserve balances with the Clearing Union and not with one another." To make sure that he was properly understood, Keynes added that "in order that sterling and dollar might not appear to compete with *bancor* for the purpose of reserve balances, the United Kingdom and the United States might agree together that they would not accept the reserve balances of other countries in excess of normal working balances except in the case of banks definitely belonging to a Sterling Area or Dollar Area group." Had Keynes's warning been heeded, the new system might have been prevented from becoming once more embroiled in difficulties stemming from the use of national currencies as international liquidity reserves.

With the benefit of hindsight we can say that the Keynes Plan was by far the better of the two competing proposals. It would have had the following advantages: (1) creation of a powerful international institution, able to supply international liquidity in response to the world's real needs; (2) avoidance of a rebirth of the gold-exchange standard in form of the emerging dollar standard; (3) emphasis on the special responsibilities of the surplus or creditor countries; and (4) stress on the primacy of domestic economic policies and on arrangements by which par values would be more or less automatically adjusted in response to changes in the debit and credit accounts of the Clearing Union.

Since it was not put into operation, we do not know what defects the Clearing Union might have developed. Possibly it could have been mismanaged in the direction of even greater worldwide inflation; possibly, too, the automatic adjustment of par values might have been too obvious, and therefore too easy to anticipate by private speculation. But these defects could have been corrected; the inflation danger, for instance, by setting realistic upper limits for *bancor* drawings, and disequilibrating speculation by making par-value adjustments still more frequent and smaller on each occasion.

The International Monetary Fund

While the International Monetary Fund follows in its main outlines the proposals of Harry D. White, it was decisively influenced by Keynes. The very fact that "monetary" replaced "stabilization" in the title of the new institution was significant; and so was the fact that the possibility of parity adjustments was more strongly emphasized. White had suggested such adjustments only "when essential to the correction of fundamental disequilibrium in a member's balance of payments." The Fund Agreement referred only to "fundamental disequilibrium" as such, opening the possibility for a much broader interpretation. For instance, one can argue that a country is in fundamental disequilibrium *domestically* owing to efforts to reach or maintain external balance. International-payments equilibrium may have been achieved at the expense of growing unemployment. The new vagueness of the concept "fundamental disequilibrium" made it possible for the followers of White and Keynes to come to an agreement which each party could interpret to its own liking.

According to Article I of the International Monetary Fund Agreement,[2] the IMF wants to promote stable exchange rates, avoid competitive exchange depreciation, and gradually eliminate foreign-exchange restrictions. The Fund's resources are available to its members, and are to help them "to correct maladjustments in their balance of payments without resorting to measures destructive of national or international prosperity."

It is significant that Article I does not yet mention that changes in par values are permitted to correct fundamental disequilibria. Obviously, this basic deviation from the gold standard was meant to be a rare event. What most experts at Bretton Woods wanted was a return to fixed parities. Even today some of the Fund's Executive Directors favor what they call the par-value system, which makes parity adjustment infrequent exceptions from the general rule of fixity.

Wanting to return to a system with fixed par values, the experts faced the problem of combining it with the new freedom that the prospective members were demanding for their domestic economic policies. If currency convertibility was to be regained and maintained, the combination of reasonably independent domestic policies with very rare par-value adjustments could be accomplished only if (1) the Fund had very substantial resources with which to sustain the deficit countries, and (2) the Fund could make surplus countries participate symmetrically in the adjustment process. Yet the Fund's resources were pitifully small when held against the quantum of reserves which the structure of the new system required, and the power to make surplus countries behave was very modest because the surplus countries were not in need of the Fund's assistance.

What the Fund did accomplish unwittingly was the growth of a new type of gold-exchange standard—the dollar standard, by which an ever-increasing deficit of the United States solved the liquidity problem which the Fund was not able to solve.

A member contributes to the Fund its own national currency and gold, the total contribution being equal to a member's "quota." Quotas are determined by such factors as a country's national income, gold holdings, and relative importance of (and fluctuations in) foreign trade. The obligatory gold contribution is "the smaller of (i) 25 percent of its quota; or (ii) ten percent of its net official holdings of gold and United States dollars." It is important to notice that voting rights in the International Monetary Fund depend on the size of the members' quotas.

A member can buy from the Fund foreign currency with its own currency, but has exhausted its purchasing rights when the Fund's holdings of its currency have reached 200 percent of its quota. Since a member may normally not buy more foreign exchange than an amount equal to 25 percent of its quota in any twelve-month period, it would take at least five years before it has exhausted its purchasing rights, assuming that it contributed originally 25 percent in gold and the rest in its own currency.

However, no member is supposed to stay in a deficit position. Since 1953 the Fund has developed the practice of concluding so-called stand-by agreements with needy members, assuring them that they may purchase from the Fund up to a specified amount provided that they in turn purchase their own currencies back from the Fund with gold-convertible currencies and within a stated period of time.

These "repurchases" are absolutely essential if the Fund is to maintain its liquidity, without which it would cease to function. If the members were not under a repurchase obligation, the assets of the Fund would soon come to consist solely of the "soft" currencies of deficit countries; that is, currencies that are not in demand. The "hard" currencies of the surplus countries would all have been sold. The Fund could buy more hard currencies with gold, but would eventually run out of gold. While the repurchase obligations of Article V are technically complicated, their meaning is clear. A deficit country must sooner or later develop a payments surplus and use specified amounts of it to help the Fund regain a more liquid position. The Fund can function only if its members do not remain permanently in deficit or surplus positions.

Since the aggregate purchasing rights of members in deficit may exceed the Fund's resources—a possibility that could not arise in Keynes's Clearing Union, where debits and credits were always equal—the Fund Agreement had to contain complicated "scarce-currency" provisions. When the Fund's supply of a member's currency no longer meets the demand, the Fund may, according to Article VII, (1) require the member to sell its currency for gold; (2) ask the member for a loan, though "no member shall be under any obligation to make such loans to the Fund"; (3) formally declare such currency as scarce and "authorize any member, after consultation with the Fund, temporarily to impose limitations on the freedom of exchange operations in the scarce currency." We see that the Fund may be forced to introduce the very exchange restrictions that it was created to abolish.

The Fund can attempt to influence the domestic economic policies of its members through its repurchase and scarce-currency provisions. For instance, it can suggest to deficit countries more restrictive monetary policies or downward adjustment of par values, while surplus members can be advised to increase foreign lending, expand their monetary circulation, or revalue upward. Naturally, the Fund is stronger when dealing with deficit countries than with surplus countries.

It would be wrong to picture the Fund as an enormous institution through which all international payments are flowing. The overwhelming amount of international payments is handled by the foreign-exchange markets without participation of the Fund. The Fund deals only with the central banks or treasuries of member countries. Transactions with the Fund are of an extraordinary nature, similar to actual flows of gold under the international gold standard.

Suppose that the Banque de France buys Japanese yen from the Fund's yen account in the central bank of Japan. The Fund's yen reserves go down, its franc account grows. The Banque de France has acquired yen for sale to French commercial banks and their customers. If we assume the existence of a fractional reserve system, in which, for instance, the French commercial banks are expected to maintain reserve deposits with the Banque de France equal to 20 percent of their own customers' demand deposits, the transaction can have a contractionist impact in the gold-standard fashion. The commercial banks, in purchasing yen from the Banque de France and selling them to their customers, find their reserve deposits and their customers' demand deposits reduced by the same amount, being thus short of required backing reserves. Strictly speaking, they have now to embark on credit contraction, reducing the monetary circulation by four times the original transaction in yen. At the same time, the Banque de France would not be supposed to help the commercial banks through lending operations. On the contrary, the Banque de France might be expected to try to regain external balance by raising the rate of interest, thus making it more expensive for the commercial banks to borrow, and inducing them to make borrowing less attractive to their own customers. The opposite would be true for Japan, where the yen paid by French importers would increase the reserves of Japanese banks in the central bank, permitting them to expand credit to their customers by a multiple amount. Japan's improved position in the Fund, in turn, should encourage the Japanese central bank to stimulate even greater monetary expansion, with the aim of reaching external equilibrium.

Looking at the members' transactions with the Fund in this way, we could be tempted to conclude that they are rather similar to the adjustment process under the gold standard. This interpretation is also suggested by the fact that a system based on a combination of (1) fixed par values, (2) convertibility, and (3) relatively modest Fund resources had to be committed to a more or less *automatic* integration of the members' domestic monetary policies.

Other considerations argue against this interpretation of the Bretton Woods system as a kind of gold mechanism. First, in the eyes of its Keynesian supporters, the Fund was expressly designed to avoid credit contraction if it should be destructive of national prosperity. Second, it is no longer to be taken for granted that surplus countries would automatically expand their monetary circulation in response to a growing creditor position in the Fund. And third, a more permissive attitude toward national economic policies made sense only if it was assumed that the Fund would permit or even demand relatively frequent changes of par values. Divergence of economic policies of the members could be combined with currency convertibility only if the rule of fixity of exchange rates was replaced by a system permitting greater flexibility.

At the time of its foundation, Keynes insisted that the Fund was "the exact opposite of the gold standard," [3] while John H. Williams remarked that it was "essentially a gold standard plan." [4] These contradictory interpretations indicate two basically different philosophies behind the new institution. The outcome was (1) that the Bretton Woods system needed far greater liquidity reserves than the Fund could provide, and was forced into shanghaiing the U.S. dollar as international money; and (2) that the system had to weather repeated international monetary crises connected with the relatively rare but substantial par-value changes.

The Fund uses gold as its most liquid asset and, until recently, as international unit of account. However, in stating that "the par value of the currency of each member shall be expressed in terms of gold as a common denominator or in terms of the United States dollar of the weight and fineness in effect on July 1, 1944," Article IV of the Fund Agreement helped push the dollar rather than gold into the role of international numéraire, in which it remained at least until August 15, 1971.

The Fund's assets were covered by a gold-value guarantee. In case of devaluation, a member had to pay to the Fund an amount in its own currency equal to the reduction of the gold value of the Fund's holdings of its currency, while in the case of upvaluation the Fund had to return to the member an equivalent amount. The principle of this guarantee will remain the same even though the Fund has now shifted to a so-called SDR standard, which will be explained in the following chapters.

In contemplating gold in the framework of the Bretton Woods system, we must beware of a common misunderstanding. Maintenance of the gold parity of the dollar "as of July 1, 1944" did not impart to the dollar the "intrinsic" value of gold. It was the other way round: the monetary policy of the United States determined the purchasing power of the dollar in terms of commodity prices. Maintenance of parity between gold and dollar, therefore, exposed gold to a continuous depreciation as commodity, because all other prices were permitted to rise in terms of dollars while the gold price stayed fixed.

The Gold-Dollar Standard

Had the functioning of the world's monetary system depended exclusively on the resources of the Fund, it would soon have become evident that these resources were far too small. The dollar shortage of the postwar years would not have been overcome. However, there was a way out of this difficulty; namely, a return to an improved gold-exchange standard.

We remember that the gold-exchange standard permits the holding of international liquidity reserves in currencies that are gold-convertible. For all practical purposes, there was, after World War II, only one country that could play the role of supplier of international liquidity reserves of this type. The gold-exchange standard became a gold-dollar standard.

The most important difference between the new system and the old gold-exchange standard was that the United States acted, on the whole, more responsible than she and other gold-standard countries had acted between the wars. The United States willingly played the role as leader in international monetary affairs, that is, she acted as what the Germans call *Leitwährungsland,* the country with the guiding currency. What the United States had not been willing to undertake within the framework of a broadly conceived international institution like the Keynesian Clearing Union, she did through her direct efforts to help other nations return to currency convertibility.

After World War II, the international-payments problem presented itself as an enormous dollar gap. Before normal payments relationships could begin, the Western market economies and Japan had to be reconstructed. In this process the United States played a decisive role. No wonder, then, that the dollar appeared as good as, or even better than, gold. The United States was the richest country, the dollar was amply backed by gold, and was, it seemed, not in the slightest danger of ever having to be devalued. Furthermore, foreign-held dollar balances earned interest and were, therefore, more attractive than sterile gold reserves.

In spite of large surpluses in commodity trade, the United States showed continued payments deficits owing to her role as key-currency country. Substantial amounts of dollars which flowed abroad as grants and loans were not used for commodity imports but kept as international liquidity reserve. These dollar balances were short-term claims on the United States and, technically speaking, a balance-of-payments deficit. In official hands, they were even convertible into gold. However, since international liquidity reserves were desperately needed and the dollar was considered preferable to gold, the convertibility of dollars into gold seemed not to endanger the U.S. payments position, and all countries were glad to increase their dollar balances.

The picture changed around 1958 when, after the reconstruction, foreign-held dollar balances increased beyond what some countries considered desirable amounts. For them the dollar shortage turned into a dollar glut. The United States deficit became problematic.

Why, then, did the United States not simply reduce the dollar outflow? Loans and grants could have been cut. Alternatively, if these capital flows were considered politically indispensable, why were they not transferred in real terms through an increased export of commodities and services? Furthermore, why did the countries that were experiencing a dollar glut continue to increase their dollar balances? Why did they not simply import more by spending the dollars they did not want to keep? Since the dollar glut could have been attacked from both sides, that is, by the United States as well as by the surplus countries, there was much opportunity here for differences of opinion and political conflict. Each party could argue that the other was guilty and should do something to correct the situation.

If the dollar is used as international unit of account and all parities are fixed in dollars, each central bank must maintain a completely elastic supply of, and demand for, U.S. dollars at the official par value of the national currency. When Germany finds that in her foreign-exchange market the supply of dollars exceeds the demand, the Bundesbank must buy dollars to prevent an appreciation of the mark in terms of dollars. On the other hand, should the demand for dollars exceed the supply, the Bundesbank would have to sell dollars out of its reserves. Sales of dollars reduce reserves and cannot be continued indefinitely; purchases of dollars with marks, on the other hand, can continue indefinitely, but have the effect of increasing the German monetary circulation and cause inflation.

Again we can note the connection between international payments and national monetary policies. A deficit country could stop the loss of dollar reserves by monetary contraction, but may not want to consider a policy that would increase unemployment. In the opposite case, a surplus country could stop inflation, caused by the purchasing of surplus dollars, but may refuse to raise interest rates or taxes to compensate for a situation for which it does not feel responsible and which, for the time being, offers all the advantages of undervaluation. Yet both deficit and surplus countries may feel inclined to argue that the United States should see to it that the world supply of international liquidity in the form of dollar balances is neither too small nor too large, even though between themselves they could not agree on what the ideal dollar supply ought to be.

Countries that are suffering from a dollar glut like to say that they are forced to import inflation from the United States. The implication seems to be that the United States follows inflationary policies at home that are worse than those of other countries, and that this inflation stimulates U.S. imports and harms U.S. exports, and thus causes the dollar glut in other countries. Then, having to buy dollars to avoid an appreciation of their own currencies, surplus countries are pushed into the unwelcome position of having to expand their domestic monetary circulation. The balance-of-payments deficit of the United States seems to transmit the U.S. inflation to other countries.

However, even if the price level in the United States were to rise more slowly than in the surplus countries, as it frequently has, "imported" inflation could still plague the latter. The U.S. deficit need not be caused by a U.S. price inflation. It can, for instance, be the result of large unilateral-aid payments to less-developed countries or of huge private capital flows. An excess supply of dollars in Europe, for instance, could result from U.S. military aid to Thailand, while increased private foreign investments could be induced by the desire of U.S. corporations to locate production facilities inside the European Common Market. These policy decisions need have nothing to do with differential rates of inflation. Nevertheless, the dollar-glut countries may object. They can argue that official or private U.S. decisions in which they, the surplus countries, have no voice, produce deficits for the United States and that, owing to the very nature of the present international monetary system, the absorption of excess dollars by the surplus countries amounts to the automatic financing of American policies (and deficits) by other nations. The dollar-glut countries appear to be captive members of a dollar standard whose benefits go one-sidedly to the United States, which enjoys (or at least enjoyed in the past) the unique advantage of being able to borrow automatically in any desired amount, as long as the surplus countries must buy dollars in the process of maintaining their official parity.

Some observers have suggested that the international dollar standard relieved the United States of the necessity of considering the effect of her domestic policies on her external balance. Being able to finance deficits automatically, the United States was actually encouraged to follow unsound policies. This situation would have been impossible had payments deficits led to a prompt outflow of gold from the United States. As we shall see, some of these critics come to the conclusion that the world should go back to the gold standard after having first arranged for a sufficient supply of gold reserves by a massive general upvaluation of gold.

The criticism of the gold-dollar standard by the dollar-glut countries tended to overstate the advantages to the United States as the nation that can finance external deficits by automatic borrowing. Against this argument we must hold the fact that the United States maintained, up to August 15,

1971, a fixed gold parity, while all other members of the Fund could correct fundamental disequilibria by changing the par value of their currencies in relation to the dollar. It was not stated in the Fund Agreement that the gold value of the dollar would have to remain fixed, but the special position of the dollar as pivot of the system, as the world's unit of account and major liquidity reserve, seemed to make it practically impossible to contemplate a dollar devaluation in terms of gold.

As many countries devalued their currencies, sometimes substantially and repeatedly, while up to the fall of 1969 no upvaluations took place, the U.S. dollar became more and more overvalued. Surplus countries which refused to upvalue their currencies found themselves in an increasingly favorable competitive position. The International Monetary Fund, though eager to eliminate competitive exchange depreciation, did nothing to stop the practice of surplus countries to maintain undervalued parities. Refusal by the surplus countries to upvalue hurt the deficit countries. However, with the exception of the United States, they could at least correct their competitive position by devaluation. The brunt of the impact of distorted parities, therefore, was felt by the United States.

It is true, of course, that the involvement of the United States in international trade is smaller than that of many other countries in terms of her national income. But this very fact can be used to support the argument that the United States could not be expected to let the tail wag the dog. U.S. monetary and fiscal policies, in other words, could not primarily be used to defend an artificially overvalued dollar at the cost of increasing unemployment.

Germany, Japan, and other surplus countries saw the problem in a different light. They had made an impressive effort to reconstruct their economies and had, once again, become very competitive in the world market. It was this competitive effort that the United States had been selflessly eager to support in the early postwar period. When their reconstruction efforts succeeded, it was only natural that the European countries and Japan were proud of their achievement, and not eager to admit that part of the success had been due to the artificial advantage that their main competitor was disadvantaged by an overvalued dollar.

Since monetary stability is generally considered preferable to inflation, it was natural for surplus countries to argue that the correction of an international-payments disequilibrium should be brought about by the toning down of the inflationary policies of the deficit countries rather than by a stepped-up money circulation in the surplus countries. Nevertheless, the surplus countries had to upvalue sooner or later if they wanted to continue their anti-inflation policies. As we saw, a surplus country maintains its fixed parity by buying, with newly issued domestic money, the foreign-currency earnings that cannot be absorbed by the private foreign-exchange market at the official parity. These purchases cause the phenomenon of imported inflation, which may finally convince the administration that an upvaluation cannot be postponed much longer, even though the export sector of the economy may still be violently opposed to a policy that ends an artificial export advantage.

It is interesting to note that for similar reasons the opponents of up-valuation were for a long time reluctant to suggest a devaluation of the dollar. They suggested that the United States mend her ways, but they did not like it too much when she really went ahead and tried to put her house in order, either by devaluation or by more conservative monetary policies.

The United States, as the main supplier of international liquidity, could never hope that her policies would meet with the simultaneous approval of all other countries. Most countries are still suffering from a shortage of in-ternational liquidity, and would be hurt if the United States followed one-sidedly the advice of the dollar-glut countries. In other words, the United States was, and still is, in the not-very-enviable position that no policy she decides to follow could simultaneously satisfy all members of the system. This fact argues strongly for an international monetary system in which the supply of international liquidity can be divorced from the domestic economic policies of one dominant country.

Bretton Woods and the Dollar Crisis

With the growing dollar glut, the important element of confidence entered the international-payments picture. Was the dollar really as strong as, or even stronger than, gold? Had not the decline of U.S. gold reserves and the increase of foreign-held dollar balances undermined the gold backing of the dollar? Was it not possible, after all, that the once mighty dollar would have to be devalued by raising the dollar price of gold?

The argument was interesting, and frightening. If gold stock and gold production are inadequate to take care of the total demand for international liquidity reserves; if the resources of the Fund, too, are inadequate; if the continuous growth of foreign-held dollar balances implies a permanently growing U.S. deficit; if a permanently growing deficit lowers the world's confidence in the dollar; and if confidence is still further lowered by a deteriorating net-reserve position of the United States (that is, the ratio of foreign-held dollar balances to official U.S. gold reserves)—then, it was concluded, the system is bound to collapse someday with consequences even worse than those of the breakdown of the gold-exchange standard before World War II.[5]

The impact of August 15, 1971, when gold convertibility of official foreign-held dollar balances was abandoned, and the consequences of successive dollar devaluations, were less serious than these fears suggested. True, the system was crisis-prone. But these crises stemmed mainly from the fact that, with more or less predictable major parity changes in cases of fundamental disequilibrium, disturbing capital movements from deficit into surplus countries had to take place. With enormous dollar balances, international monetary crises had invariably to turn into dollar crises.

Nevertheless, the world finds it difficult to release the dollar from its various international functions, mainly because an adequate substitute is not yet available.

International Liquidity and Special Drawing Rights

The Supply of Liquidity

The Bretton Woods system, in which the par values of the members' currencies are subject to only rare but substantial changes, was bound to lead to repeated international monetary crises. Each parity adjustment took place in an atmosphere of emergency, since the basic condition for changes in par values was the existence of an often highly visible fundamental disequilibrium which produced self-aggravating hot-money movements in anticipation of parity changes. The situation was rendered even worse by the fact that superimposed on the par-value system was a dollar standard in which (up to August 15, 1971) official dollar balances were convertible into gold, while the dollar served as intervention currency, liquidity reserve, and international unit of account.

The dollar-gold parity remained fixed from 1944 to 1971, while all other Fund members were free to adjust their parities. Furthermore, since most of these adjustments were devaluations, the U.S. dollar became increasingly overvalued. Overvaluation of the dollar intensified the growing external deficit of the United States and the deterioration of her net-reserve position, thereby promoting the fear that the dollar's par value and official gold convertibility might not be maintained indefinitely.

Thus the stage was set not only for localized payments crises, in which the par values of individual countries came to be adjusted, but for a scenario in which local crises often became dollar crises because practically any uncertainty tended to reawaken fears of a potential dollar devaluation.

Each international-payments crisis produced ad hoc emergency measures that permitted the shoring-up of the system until the next fundamental disequilibrium appeared on the horizon. Some of these measures contained new constructive ideas for permanent monetary cooperation. However, the total of all arrangements could hardly be called a system anymore, if by system we mean an interdependent group of items forming a unified whole.

It has become customary to subdivide the international-payments problem into the three issues adjustment, liquidity, and confidence.[1] This subdivision is useful, provided that the interdependence between the three issues is duly considered. Obviously, the demand for liquidity reserves depends mainly on the quality of the adjustment mechanism of the system.

35

Once we improve the adjustment process we may expect a decrease in the demand for liquidity. In the extreme case of freely floating exchange rates, no official liquidity reserves would be needed.

At first the scene was dominated by the liquidity problem. The confidence problem emerged only gradually, with the dollar glut and the deteriorating net-reserve position of the United States. The adjustment problem was neglected, unless we consider the rare and substantial changes of par values, which were characteristic for the system as a satisfactory solution, or assume that the gold mechanism continued to function under the International Monetary Fund. Up to the 1970 Report of the Executive Directors of the IMF on *The Role of Exchange Rates in the Adjustment of International Payments* more frequent adjustments of par values were not seriously discussed, with the result that a solution of international payments problems was mainly sought in terms of increased liquidity creation.

However, a basic difference of opinion existed between those who felt that the system did not provide enough liquidity, and others who felt that the system created too much liquidity and thereby eliminated the discipline on which the gold standard had relied. Representatives of surplus countries tend to argue that the world's liquidity reserves are already *too large,* as evidenced by inflationary pressures exerted on their economies by growing official dollar balances and the inconvenience of having to fight imported inflation. Experience has shown that surplus countries upvalue only under extreme conditions. Deficit countries, then, will have to bear most of the adjustment burden, and accordingly will always tend to the opinion that not only their own but world reserves in general are *too small.*

The demand for international liquidity has a psychological dimension which makes it even harder to find the optimum supply of liquidity reserves. Surplus countries gradually come to regard a substantial liquidity reserve as a proud achievement and a comfortable buffer should the external balance reverse itself. As international reserves get more unequally distributed, the demand for reserves increases, because the surplus countries become accustomed to huge reserves and try to hold on to them while the deficit countries try as hard as they can to improve their inadequate liquidity position.

Arguments against greater liquidity were vigorously put forward by experts who wanted to maintain discipline in the system. These arguments have the merit of consistency but the disadvantage of being politically unrealistic, resting as they do on the assumption that only a combination of fixed parities with limited reserves would force recalcitrant governments into correct monetary behavior. According to this view, too much liquidity undermines "appropriate" economic behavior and produces external disequilibria, which lead to still more liquidity creation.

Generalizing, we can say that it will be very difficult to come to a satisfactory compromise concerning the optimum supply of world liquidity reserves for the following reasons:

1. No real answer is possible before an improved adjustment mechanism has been established and has given evidence that it can deal effectively with balance-of-payments disequilibria. Adjustment, not liquidity, is the primary problem.

2. Surplus and deficit countries will always tend to disagree on this issue until surplus and deficit positions are reversed much more frequently through a well-functioning adjustment process.

3. The discipline argument will continue to oppose insistence that domestic economic policies be given sufficient leeway.

4. Each member's attitude will depend on the degree of its involvement in international trade. The greater the foreign-trade sector in comparison with the Gross National Product, the greater should be the willingness to cooperate.

Even if it were possible to arrive at an acceptable compromise concerning the total or world supply of international liquidity reserves, it would still be necessary to maintain a reasonable distribution of these reserves among the members of the system. To put it differently, we must prevent the building up of permanent deficit and surplus positions. Here we meet again with the adjustment problem. The connection between liquidity and adjustment lies in the mechanism by which changes in a member's reserves induce certain actions to regain external balance. Changes in liquidity reserves may lead to changes in the member's monetary policy or else to an adjustment of the par value of its currency—always assuming that convertibility is being maintained.

If pressure is to be exerted on members to put their external balance in order, the supply of additional liquidity reserves to deficit countries will be made conditional, that is, it will depend on certain repayment provisions. The system should even make the accumulation of excessive liquidity reserves contingent on special actions designed to eliminate this surplus. If liquidity reserves are to be had unconditionally, the connection between liquidity and adjustment is severed and no adjustment mechanism is then trying to influence the long-term distribution of world reserves.

We can divide liquidity reserves into those whose supply can be regulated and those whose supply is haphazard. The former category includes reserves created by the International Monetary Fund or arranged between the central banks of the system, the latter comprise gold and key-currency (mainly dollar) balances. The gold supply for reserve purposes is, as we shall see, at present limited to a more or less fixed amount under a so-called two-tier arrangement by which the size of officially held gold reserves has been brought under temporary control; and much thought is given to arrangements that attempt to deal with the so-called dollar overhang. But the main interest concerning conscious management of future additions to world liquidity centers now, as we shall see, on the Fund's creation of special drawing rights (SDRs).

It is correct to say that in the past the supply of gold and U.S. dollars was haphazard in the sense that nobody was able to regulate these sources of international liquidity consciously and with the intention of maintaining optimal liquidity reserves. This may change. Later we shall have to study proposals that might decisively alter the international monetary role of gold. Similarly, the problem of foreign-held dollar balances must be clarified when the world's monetary system is being reconstructed. Theoretically at least, both gold and dollar could be demonetized internationally to make room for a new synthetic reserve asset whose supply and distribution would be guided by an improved process of international monetary cooperation.

For the time being we are still far from such a system. IMF resources are too small to supply all the needed liquidity reserves, even though efforts have been made to increase international liquidity within the framework of the Fund. These efforts concern: first, repeated increases of the members' quotas; second, the general arrangements to borrow (GAB); and third, and most important, the creation of special drawing rights (SDRs). The following discussions are interested in the potentialities of these techniques rather than in their past effects, which to date have been small when compared with the supply of international liquidity out of sources that are not under the Fund's jurisdiction.

As seen at Bretton Woods, an increase in international liquidity could always be achieved by a decision to raise the quotas of the members. Because of repeated quota increases and the growing number of members, the aggregate of quotas amounted to the equivalent of $29,169 million at the end of April 1973 as against $7600 million in 1946.[2] To evaluate these figures it must be remembered, however, that the liquidity that the Fund can provide via regular drawings is limited by the Fund's holdings of gold and member currencies that are in demand. Furthermore, it must not be forgotten that the Fund's regular resources may not even be sufficient within the frame of reference of the Fund itself whatever their size, considering that any general increase in quotas does not remove the asymmetrical structure of the Fund, which can lead to a scarce-currency situation and the introduction of exchange controls.

We have seen that normal or traditional drawings are subject to strict limitations, to progressive charges, and to repurchase obligations—conditions clearly meant to induce the drawing country to undertake speedy rectification of its external balance by appropriate domestic policies. However, the Fund has relaxed these strict rules somewhat by its standby agreements and to an even larger extent for primary producing countries. The latter can draw on the Fund's resources to meet payments deficits arising out of export shortfalls, provided that the latter are largely attributable to circumstances beyond the control of the member and provided further that the member is willing to cooperate with the Fund in seeking appropriate solutions for its balance-of-payments difficulties. The main point is that while with regard to these countries the so-called tranche limitations have been liberalized, their drawings remain strictly conditional. These exceptions prove the rule that "in a world in which the adjustment process is still largely unregulated by international agreement, the credit tranche policies perform part of the task, although only for members in balance of payments deficit." [3]

According to the Fund Agreement only the first or so-called gold tranche (equal to a member's original gold contribution) is to be used unconditionally. Similarly, any surplus country can use its creditor position in the Fund (the so-called super gold tranche) to purchase other currencies unconditionally. But the Fund cannot make the members' drawing rights in the credit tranches unconditional, because the Fund's own liquidity depends, as we saw, on the members' repurchases. Furthermore, the Fund's power to induce adjustments in the members' domestic policies would decrease to the degree that a liberalization in the use of the credit tranches were to take place.

The Fund's structural asymmetry and the resulting scarce-currency provisions could have been avoided had the experts at Bretton Woods been willing to make loans to the Fund by surplus countries obligatory. But Article VII declares expressly that "no member shall be under any obligation to make such loans to the Fund." In 1961 negotiations concerning a borrowing arrangement took place between the Fund and the so-called Group of Ten (consisting of Belgium, Canada, France, Germany, Italy, Japan, The Netherlands, Sweden, the United Kingdom, and the United States), in which the Ten agreed "to stand ready to lend their currencies to the Fund up to specified amounts when the Fund and these countries considered that supplementary sources were needed by the Fund to forestall or cope with an impairment of the international monetary system." [4] Even these general arrangements to borrow (GABs), however, are not an absolute guarantee for elimination of the Fund's structural asymmetry. First, because the participants are still only obligated to "consider" a requested loan, and second, because the Ten meant the new facility for their own exclusive use.

The third method used to increase international liquidity through the

International Monetary Fund, the creation of special drawing rights (SDRs) constitutes a major breakthrough in international monetary thinking, and is by far the most important development since Bretton Woods.

Special Drawing Rights

The plan to create SDRs was the result of a lengthy discussion. The problem was how international liquidity reserves could be consciously created and could, to that extent, become independent of the haphazardness which characterized additions to monetary gold reserves and foreign-held dollar balances. Besides, many members of the Fund were dissatisfied with the strictly conditional nature of the traditional drawing rights in the credit tranches—otherwise the whole problem of additions to liquidity reserves might have been solved simply by speeding up the process of quota increases and making it independent of additional gold contributions.

Some experts tried to solve the dollar problem by the use of "multiple currency reserves." [5] Other major countries (for instance the other members of the Group of Ten) would then have shared with the United States the advantages and disadvantages of a key-currency status; and the new arrangements could have helped avoid the continuing deterioration of the net-reserve position of the United States. The monetary authorities of the Ten could have agreed to hold the foreign-exchange component of their liquidity reserves in a prearranged "mix" of currencies, and could have undertaken to raise or lower the whole foreign-exchange component in relation to gold to achieve a desired total of liquidity reserves.

The major drawback of a multicurrency arrangement is that it exposes the international payments system to frequent shifts in reserve assets, that is, to disequilibrating capital movements, unless ways can be found to make the different currencies completely substitutable. It is doubtful that this condition can be met, considering interest-rate differentials and the possibility of parity adjustments.

Shifts between national currencies could be avoided by the creation of an artificial reserve unit. The members of the Group of Ten, for instance, could put specified amounts of their currencies into the International Monetary Fund in exchange for value-guaranteed Fund deposits, and the latter would then serve as liquidity reserve. The limitation to important countries is to be explained by the fact that, psychologically speaking, only the currencies of strong or major countries would seem fit to serve as backing for this addition to international liquidity reserves. France even suggested the creation of a collective reserve unit (CRU), which would have been distributed among the Ten in proportion to their respective stocks of gold.

More important, however, than this implied notion of some kind of gold backing was France's insistence that the other members of the international monetary system would then have to borrow CRUs under reasonably strict conditions.

Most participants in this discussion finally favored a radically different approach, namely the creation of a new reserve asset that would instantly and unconditionally increase the liquidity reserves of all Fund members.

The special drawing rights that were approved by the International Monetary Fund in September 1967 in Rio rest on the following principles: [6]

1. All members of the Fund have the privilege of being "participants" in the new scheme, but no member is bound to participate in it or in any future allocations of SDRs.

2. SDRs are not backed by national currencies, but they carry essentially the same gold guarantee as the general accounts of the Fund. They are used only between central banks.

3. The decision to create a given amount of SDRs is made by a majority of 85 percent of the voting power of the members of the Fund on the basis of a proposal by the managing director, concurred in by the executive directors. The voting power depends on the members' quotas.

4. SDRs are allocated to participating members in proportion to their quotas. *The participants do not incur a corresponding debt.* SDRs are similar to gold in that they are a generally acceptable reserve asset *without being anybody's legal debt.* Foreign-held dollar balances, by contrast, are a debt of the United States, and repayment of this debt extinguishes reserve assets. The amount of SDRs can never decrease, except in the unlikely case of a cancellation of the whole scheme.

5. A participating member can use its SDRs to meet legitimate balance-of-payments needs, but not for the sole purpose of changing the composition of its official liquidity reserves.

6. The use of SDRs is unconditional, with the one exception that the participant must maintain an average balance of SDRs equal to 30 percent of the net cumulative allocation during each basic period of five years. A participant which has reduced its SDR balance below 30 percent must "reconstitute" it, that is, must purchase SDRs to that extent with convertible currencies. But even in this case SDRs are only transferred and not destroyed.

7. When a participant desires to purchase convertible currencies with SDRs, the Fund tells one or more participants to transfer convertible currencies to the drawing participant in exchange for SDRs. Criteria for the Fund's decision which countries are to sell convertible currencies for SDRs are (a) strong reserve positions and (b) relatively low ratios of their SDR holdings to total reserves.

8. The obligations of surplus countries are limited, however. No participant is obliged to hold more than three times its own cumulative allocations of SDRs, but may agree to hold more.

9. A participant pays an interest charge of 1½ percent per annum on its net allocation of SDRs and receives an interest payment of 1½ percent on the amount of its SDR holdings, so that, on balance, only a net user of SDRs pays interest while a participant receives interest on SDR holdings in excess of the amount of its original allocation.

10. The SDR scheme can have special meaning for the United States or other key-currency countries. The United States may, for instance, transfer SDRs to participants that desire to reduce their dollar balances.

The SDR arrangements have the advantage of permitting the deliberate creation of a reserve asset that is equal to gold in the sense that with gold it shares "the feature of being internationally acceptable in exchange for national currency without being a legal debt of any nation, institution, or organization." [7] Compared with gold the SDRs have the advantage that their supply can be regulated in response to the demand for liquidity, provided that the correct decision is made and supported by 85 percent of the voting power of the participants. To make the right decision will be difficult. We must remember the many differences of opinion that stand in the way of a sound compromise on optimal liquidity supply and the fact that the SDR allocations will have to try to compensate for the haphazard behavior of the other major reserve assets.

An advantage of SDR creation over a general upvaluation of gold as source of increased liquidity is that SDRs are distributed among *all* participants. Gold, on the other hand, still has the psychological advantage of being in the minds of many observers the reserve asset of last resort. Its value seems to be intrinsic and to be actually supporting the SDRs, which enjoy a gold-value guarantee. The truth is, of course, that the value of gold, too, depends, in the end, on the monetary demand for gold and arbitrary decisions concerning the par values of currencies in terms of gold. If the future role of SDRs depends on political decisions, so does the future monetary role of gold. Seen quantitatively, gold is still the by far more important reserve asset, and it is conceivable, though perhaps not at all likely that a general upvaluation will put gold once more into the dominant position.

SDRs and the Adjustment Process

The decision to create SDRs was a remarkable step, which may have great importance for the future of the international monetary system. Nevertheless, the new scheme has one serious drawback. Where past efforts have tried to put newly created institutions and arrangements to work in an effort to solve the adjustment problem, the SDR scheme is left with only weak remnants of adjustment features. Indeed, the main, and to some the most attractive, feature of the new arrangement is the replacement of conditional by unconditional reserve assets. No doubt from the standpoint of many participants there are great advantages connected with the automatic distribution and ownership of the newly created reserves. For the right purpose the owner can use SDRs at will and has nothing to repay, at least not for the first 70 percent of the allocations. These allocations are not loans, they are gifts. There are practically no obligations connected with SDRs designed to engender disciplined behavior on the part of the participants.

In comparing SDRs with Keynes's *bancor* and with the regular drawing rights of the Fund, we notice substantial differences. The members of the Clearing Union would have been obliged to take corrective action when their *bancor* deficits or surpluses in the Union would grow. While the total of *bancor* balances could not have decreased (just as the total of SDRs cannot fall), the distribution of *bancor* among members was supposed to be subject to a corrective mechanism to avoid continuous one-sided deviations from the original position in the Clearing Union. Similarly, the repurchase and scarce-currency provisions of the Fund had the function of maintaining the liquidity of the Fund's resources. In both the Clearing Union and the IMF the members had to achieve long-run balance-of-payments equilibrium. Otherwise, operations in both institutions would have come to a halt for the lack of available liquidity reserves. All *bancor* balances or drawing rights would eventually have been in the hands of the surplus countries.

The members of the Clearing Union or the Fund were expected to change either their domestic monetary policies or the par values of their currencies. Neither institution accepted the creation of repeated instalments of drawing rights as alternative to the adjustment process.

The SDR arrangements lack the adjustment features of the older schemes, at least as far as the first 70 percent of SDR allocations are concerned. Unless an adjustment mechanism is provided *in some other and independent way,* we must expect, therefore, that the newly allocated SDRs will flow from deficit to surplus participants with no regular backflow.

It is true that the IMF will see to it that the SDRs are getting distributed as equally as possible among those participants which have convertible currencies to sell. But this attempt at distributing the SDRs evenly among surplus countries does not solve the problem of their distribution as between deficit and surplus members. As in all payments systems that are expected to function, the participants should constantly move from deficit back to surplus positions; yet the SDR scheme does nothing to accomplish a continuous striving for external equilibrium among all participants.

The consequence will be that the deficit members of the system will cry—and now vote—for more liquidity in the form of larger SDR creations, while the surplus countries among the participants will suffer from the same surfeit of reserves which led to the phenomenon of imported inflation. Unless, therefore, the SDR scheme is soon followed by a thorough and successful reconstruction of the adjustment process, it can lead to serious difficulties. New reserve assets which are magnetically drawn into the reserves of the surplus countries do not contribute to a permanent solution of the world's liquidity problem. We cannot even assume that under such conditions new SDR allocations will be forthcoming for very long. New allocations would be stopped by the surplus countries under the 85 percent majority rule.

In a system characterized by stubborn external disequilibria, allocations of SDRs to surplus countries seem to be a waste of international liquidity reserves. It was held against the key-currency system that it gave unlimited borrowing rights to the United States. The SDR scheme can be similarly criticized for handing SDRs over to surplus countries which have no need for them. Both systems can be blamed for carrying coals to Newcastle.

Money creation, whether domestic or international, means creation of additional spending power. When newly created SDRs are spent they finance an import surplus, which is a net gain for the importing country, which has not incurred a debt in the process. The export countries, on the other hand, will not only find themselves with their own SDR allocations for which they have no present use, but also with earned SDRs, which will tend to have an inflationary effect owing to the reduction of the domestic commodity supply implicit in export surpluses and the increased liquidity of their monetary systems.

These effects would be even stronger if we followed the suggestion that all newly created SDRs should be allocated exclusively to less-developed countries. Assuming that the world needs an addition of, say, 5 billion SDRs to its liquidity reserve, it is often asked why this whole amount should not be given to those who are in need of development aid. Coals would not be carried to Newcastle and international reserves would be more effectively increased than if an identical amount is distributed among poor and rich alike. The answer is, of course, that as long as the system lacks a functioning adjustment mechanism, the new SDRs will simply permit the financing of bigger deficits, and will put surplus countries under still greater inflationary pressure.

The Bretton Woods experts considered it so vital to distinguish clearly between the short-time financing of payments deficits and the long-term financing of development that they created two independent institutions:

the International Monetary Fund and the International Bank for Reconstruction and Development. Under no condition were the drawing rights of the Fund to deteriorate into long-term financing of development. Investment of borrowed funds in fixed capital goods implies illiquidity. Since it was essential for the Fund to be kept liquid through regular repurchases, the members were not supposed to use the resources of the Fund for development finance.

While the idea of handing over all newly created SDRs to developing countries seems eminently attractive to the latter's representatives, it must be stated that there is no logical connection between SDR creation and development aid. Development aid should not be "linked" with the world's need for additional liquidity. It would become politically impossible to arrive at a reasonable figure for SDR creation if the decision were dominated by the need for development assistance. The outcome could be that liquidity creation would be excessive, while total long-term development financing through foreign sources might not nearly be large enough. Furthermore, the dispute could affect other issues, for instance the introduction of a better adjustment mechanism. The developing countries might want to make a positive vote for, say, a gliding band dependent on what they consider a satisfactory creation of SDRs.

If we want to solve the international liquidity problem of the future via the creation of SDRs, it is more necessary than ever that a better adjustment process be provided, an adjustment process that works even in a regime with unconditional drawing rights.

5

The Basic Weakness of the Par-Value System

Three Roads to Adjustment

By "adjustment policies" we refer to measures that help achieve equilibrium in international payments. There are three ways in which this can be done under conditions of free currency convertibility.

First, adjustment can be achieved by integrating the national monetary policies of the members of the international payments system. The prototype of this adjustment process is the pre-1914 gold mechanism. In its pure form it rested on permanently fixed parities and convertibility of national currencies into gold. Gold reserves permitted the temporary financing of payments deficits. A loss or gain of gold induced contractionist or expansionist monetary policies. Basically, this mechanism is independent of gold, however. Essential is the connection of a loss of international liquidity reserves (of whichever kind) with a relative contraction of the domestic monetary circulation, and the linking of an excess accumulation of reserves with a relative monetary expansion. Reference to "relative" is important, since the needed degree of domestic contraction or expansion depends on the average behavior of the other members of the system. In particular, it may be sufficient for a deficit country to tone down its rate of inflation rather than engineer a deflation (that is, an absolute fall of wages and prices), provided that the rest of the world, too, is suffering from creeping inflation. In a system of worldwide inflation, a monetary adjustment mechanism can be based on the application of different rates of inflation, average inflation indicating normal monetary behavior as far as international payments equilibrium is concerned.

Second, adjustment can be achieved, and currency convertibility maintained, by a payments system with freely floating exchange rates that dispenses altogether with the fixing of official par values. The central banks of the member countries stay out of the foreign-exchange markets, and the exchange rates are determined by private market forces alone. Official foreign-exchange reserves become superfluous, and international payments are continuously kept in balance. Currency depreciation in deficit countries instantly reduces prices of commodities and services for foreign buyers, stimulates exports, and raises the cost of imports, until equilibrium is achieved. Conversely, appreciations of surplus currencies reduce exports

47

and increase imports. Adjustment is achieved automatically through the working of market forces.

Third, a system with adjustable par values à la Bretton Woods tries to combine features of the two extremes. This system excludes *permanently* fixed par values and *freely* floating exchange rates. The par values are kept fixed at any given time, but are subject to change under special conditions. We saw that the compromise of Bretton Woods insists on fixed official parities but permits changes of par values in cases of fundamental disequilibria. Depending on the definition of the latter, the system of the "adjustable peg" can come close to either end of a wide spectrum of possibilities. Very rare adjustments would approach gold-standard conditions, while a more liberal interpretation of the system could lead to very frequent parity changes and thereby approach the high degree of flexibility offered by freely floating exchange rates. However, in comparison with the latter, the parities would still be kept artificially stabilized by official purchases and sales in the foreign-exchange markets. Consequently, official liquidity reserves would be increasing or decreasing, and the par value would nearly always diverge, at least slightly, from the price that free private market forces would have established.

A special area of flexibility can be established if the market rates of exchange are permitted to fluctuate between predetermined upper and lower limits, as formerly between the gold points. We shall see, furthermore, that a margin could be established within which parity changes would be permitted within certain limits per period of time, such as, for instance, 2 or 3 percent per year. Finally, exchange rates could be permitted to float, but the monetary authorities would be active in the foreign-exchange markets to maintain "orderly" market conditions, that is, to discourage disequilibrating private speculation. The floating of the exchange rate would be not free but managed.

Through the Bretton Woods compromise of the adjustable peg, the system became more flexible than it had been under the gold standard. Adjustments of international payments depended no longer exclusively on changes in the monetary policies of the member countries. External equilibrium could now be accomplished by a mixture of changes in domestic monetary policy and parity variations. Obviously, this compromise lacks the simplicity of the pure systems (with unalterably fixed parities or freely floating exchange rates), and may have lost the strict discipline built into the one without having gained the full flexibility of the other. Whether new ways of *operating* the par-value system of Bretton Woods will be able to improve the international monetary system is perhaps the most important question facing the international experts. It is the crux of the whole matter, overshadowing in importance the liquidity issue, which cannot be satisfactorily handled before the adjustment problem has been solved.

Neither permanently fixed par values nor freely floating exchange rates seem to be politically acceptable. Modern wage and employment policies exclude the one, and widespread aversion to a system without a "fixed point of reference" the other. Conceivably, there may be some success with policies aiming at permanently rigid parities for members of a regional monetary union, such as the European Monetary Union (see chapter 8). But this would still leave the question open as to how adjustments can be achieved between monetary blocs.

The Par-Value System

The concept of "fundamental disequilibrium," though crucial for the compromise of Bretton Woods, was intentionally left undefined. Practical interpretation tended, until very recently, strongly in the direction of making par-value changes very rare exceptions from the basic rule that fixed par values be maintained by all members.

In two recent reports,[1] the executive directors of the International Monetary Fund are still arguing strongly for "the par value system, based on stable, but adjustable, par values at realistic levels."[2] They are afraid of both "premature" and "unduly delayed" changes of par values, but much more of the former than the latter. The parity is seen as "a fixed point of reference which provides a useful discipline for the maintenance of financial stability domestically."[3] The executive directors point out that fixed par values have "an important influence on basic financial magnitudes in a national economy," namely, "the flow of aggregate domestic output, incomes, and spending."[4] Fixed parities, therefore, are to force responsible monetary policies upon the members of the system, by making them change these aggregates rather than the par values of their currencies. The executive directors remind us that "in many countries the authorities have regarded a stable par value as a valuable aid in maintaining domestic economic stability," and that even in countries that have not succeeded in dispensing with eventual par-value adjustment, the norm of fixity in the exchange rate has nonetheless been considered as an aid to equilibrium, both in the domestic economy and externally, because it promoted "political willingness to impose unpopular domestic restraints."[5]

These arguments lean heavily toward the conservative or gold-standard side of the adjustment spectrum, and are characteristic of the kind of thinking that produced "undue delays" in parity adjustment, and thereby caused international-payments crises. Wrong parities are artificially maintained and lead to disequilibrating capital movements and misallocations of productive resources. Nevertheless, the executive directors of the Fund try to excuse even undue delays in the elimination of over- and undervaluations with the weak argument that "where the attempt to defend the parity is ultimately unsuccessful, the psychological shock of a devaluation may promote broad support for the adoption for the necessary associated measures to curtail domestic demand." They believe that a more continuous adjustment of parities "without the trauma implicit in the act of exchange adjustment as a last resort, would exert less pressure for domestic corrective measures." [6] Here the directors take the extreme position of actually defending unduly delayed parity changes, in spite of the admission that "these delays have sometimes tended to aggravate problems of domestic economic management, and have sometimes also aggravated the external disequilibrium." [7]

It really sounds as if the executive directors recommend international monetary crises, because of their alleged beneficial aftereffects. They concede, however, that delays in parity adjustments have fostered the use of trade and payments restrictions (that is, the decline of currency convertibility) and have led to the building up of large speculative positions which played a disequilibrating role. However, these disadvantages are seen as weaknesses of the *operation* of the par-value system rather than the system itself, and are considered "as necessary costs that in the long run are outweighed by compensating advantages." [8] Fortunately, the directors are at least willing to "consider" changes by which greater flexibility of exchange rates could be achieved.

The inconsistency of the executive directors' attitude toward flexibility of exchange rates lies in their insistence that adjustments of par values ought to be considered "premature" unless the evidence of over- or undervaluation has become "substantial." By then, however, the parities have been unrealistic for a long time and much harm has already been done by preventing their prompt adjustment. Substantial disequilibria are highly visible, private speculation will anticipate coming devaluations or upvaluations, and the stage is set for an international monetary crisis.

The attempt to prevent "premature" adjustments of par values implies the ability on the part of the Fund authorities to perform the extremely difficult task of disentangling all the price-determining influences in the foreign-exchange markets, in an effort to find out which trends are likely to reverse themselves and which are not. In arguing for parity changes only in cases of fundamental disequilibrium, the executive directors acknowledge their own limitations in market analysis by admitting that they can recognize only extreme deviations of a parity from what its real market value should be. Fundamental disequilibria are permitted to develop and a wrong policy is not corrected until the very market forces that remained unheeded revolt and force the authorities to succumb after much harm has been done.

At Bretton Woods, the fear of competitive exchange depreciation was still prevalent in the experts' attitude toward flexibility of exchange rates.

This was understandable after the experiences of the interwar period. It is much less clear why this fear should still dominate the Fund's attitude in the seventies. Today, the main danger for the system stems from competitive undervaluations rather than from competitive depreciations. The Fund may have some power left in influencing the policies of deficit countries, which are in need of the Fund's help; but the Fund is still virtually powerless when surplus countries refuse to eliminate an external disequilibrium through upvaluation. Since the Fund never used the scarce-currency provisions of Article VIII, its surplus members have enjoyed the advantages of undervaluation without being publicly criticized. Continued warning against competitive exchange depreciation, and silence about competitive undervaluation, illustrate how lopsided the defense of fixed versus flexible exchange rates has become.

Fundamental Disequilibrium

If an international payments system is to combine both adjustment mechanisms, that is, coordination of national monetary policies as well as changes in par values, it must be reasonably clear when each one is to be applied. We have seen that the compromise of Bretton Woods was possible because nobody insisted on a clear definition of "fundamental disequilibrium." Keynes and his followers assumed that reasonably frequent and small changes of par values, both up and down, would take place on the basis of such criteria as surplus and deficit positions of each member with the Fund. But the majority of experts seems to have assumed with Harry D. White—and, indeed, some of today's executive directors of the Fund—that par-value changes should be avoided at almost any cost. In practice, of course, these changes could often be postponed by liquidity creation, and the latter therefore became the center of attention.

If the mistakes of the past are to be avoided, parity adjustments must become a far more regular and frequent feature of the system and must rest on criteria that are much clearer than a mere reference to an undefined fundamental disequilibrium. If a system with managed floating should be chosen, it would be necessary to determine when the exchange rates should be stabilized through official sales or purchases of foreign currencies, and when private market forces should be left free to influence the exchange rates.

The executive directors have belatedly made the attempt to explain the elusive concept of fundamental disequilibrium. They emphasize that such a state can exist even when a member enjoys external balance, since "attainment of payments balance through the use of measures destructive of national or international prosperity would clearly not comprise a durable payments equilibrium." Specifically, the Directors refer to restrictions on trade and payments or an "unacceptably high rate of inflation or artificial measures encouraging the export of capital." [9]

Difficulties of this kind will arise, say the directors, when internal and external considerations are "pulling in opposite directions as regards domestic stabilization measures," [10] and if this conflict is of a persistent nature. Then fundamental disequilibrium may be said to exist. A surplus country with full employment, for instance, which insists on maintaining an undervalued parity, will only increase its external surplus through an inflow of capital when it tries to combat inflation by raising its interest rates; a deficit country suffering from unemployment, on the other hand, can achieve more satisfactory levels of economic activity through monetary expansion, but only at the price of worsening the external deficit as long as its parity remains overvalued, since capital will tend to leave the country.

These considerations constitute progress in the analysis of fundamental disequilibrium. However, we still do not know why parity adjustments should be limited to these "dilemma cases," which would not arise at all if more frequent parity changes were permitted to take place. The very concept of fundamental disequilibrium is too rough to serve as guide for an adjustment process that tries to introduce a speedy correction of payments imbalances.

Elimination of the shortcomings of the par-value system requires far greater flexibility of exchange rates than has, up to now, been practiced by the members of the International Monetary Fund. According to the Articles of Agreement of the IMF, adjustments of parities can take place only when members can prove the existence of a situation (fundamental disequilibrium) which a well-functioning adjustment mechanism should have avoided. In permitting par-value changes only when the par values have become evidently unrealistic, the Bretton Woods system has fostered faulty resource allocations and disequilibrating capital movements. Yet, simultaneously, the par-value system removed the discipline of permanently fixed parities, thus leaving international payments without the benefit of either one of the two basic adjustment mechanisms, concentrating instead on measures by which international liquidity could be increased, so as to tide deficit countries from one unduly delayed devaluation to the next.

Fixed Versus Flexible Exchange Rates

Since many officials and practitioners in the international-payments field are still convinced that fixed par values are good and floating exchange rates bad, it is advisable to discuss the main arguments for fixity and flexibility before undertaking a more detailed study of recent proposals for increased flexibility.

The oldest argument for fixed parities states that flexible exchange rates are bad for monetary discipline. This reasoning made sense in connection with the permanently fixed parities of the gold-standard system, particularly, as long as international liquidity was strictly limited to gold reserves. However, the present par-value system with adjustable parities cannot be defended with this argument.

First, the par-value system dispenses with permanently fixed parities. Clearly, then, as soon as the members of the system know that they can offset high rates of inflation by corresponding devaluations, they can no longer be counted on to maintain the monetary discipline which was the essence of the gold-standard game.

Second, what discipline the par-value system might have gained from the temporary fixing of parities was partially lost through excessive liquidity creation via foreign-held dollar balances.

Third, limiting itself to very rare parity changes, the par-value system actually deprived itself of a major disciplining device. Even the executive directors of the Fund admit that pressure to stop an inflation may be less under fixed par values "than if the real cost of inflation were exposed to the public at large through a depreciated exchange rate." [11] The public recognizes a depreciation and its impact on import prices much more readily than variations in official liquidity reserves.

Another group of arguments against flexible exchange rates concerns the fact that they allegedly promote insecurity in international economic transactions. To many observers it seems obvious that exchange-rate variations add an extra element of risk to business deals which cross national boundaries. Advocates of fixed par values invariably picture a regime with floating exchange rates as one in which currency speculation leads to excessive exchange-rate fluctuations. However, there is no reason why this should be so. Only when fundamental disequilibria have been permitted to develop under fixed par values, and floating exchange rates are finally used to find realistic exchange rates, will extreme price changes mirror a very unstable situation. But then the par-value system with its "undue delays" was at fault, and not the floating of exchange rates, which had to be resorted to to reestablish equilibrium.

Why floating should produce wild price gyrations under reasonably normal conditions is hard to understand. Moderate variations should normally suffice. It is, after all, the very purpose of price movements to induce prompt adjustment of supply and demand. Nevertheless, Ragnar Nurkse and others have argued that freely fluctuating exchange rates "call for constant shifts of domestic factors of production between export and home market industries, shifts which may be disturbing and wasteful." [12] These are the very shifts that the executive directors of the Fund try to avoid by preventing "premature" adjustments of parities. What they achieved, however, were unduly delayed parity changes, which produced major misallocations of resources and international payments crises.

There are several reasons why relatively mild variations of exchange rates or frequent but small parity adjustments are not likely to lead to disturbing and wasteful shifts of resources.

First of all, private speculation in foreign exchange markets may tend to be equilibrating. Suppose that the exchange rate of a deficit country depreciates. Adjustment in real terms, that is, in imports and exports of commodities, will take some time. We can assume, therefore, that the exchange rate will tend to fall more in the short than in the long run. This is the reason for the fear that trade transactions might overreact. We have to consider, however, that currency speculation would tend to exert an equalizing effect, because "the tendency for the exchange rate to fall further initially than ultimately offers an opportunity to make a profit by buying the currency now and reselling it later at a higher price." [13] In this way, the foreign-exchange market can protect itself against exaggerated price variations and make it unnecessary for the authorities to try to maintain "orderly" rates. The exchange rate of the deficit country is kept reasonably stable, and unnecessary shifts of productive resources are avoided.

Changes in resource allocation are always opposed by special interests because they cause temporary inconvenience and some unemployment. Resentment against these changes may easily turn against exchange rate variations, which seem to be their cause. But this attitude confuses symptoms and causes. By keeping the par values fixed, we do not make the real causes of price changes go away; we permit them to continue to work. We stabilize exchange rates or maintain parities, but at the expense of changes in domestic economic policies which, at least in dilemma cases, may be creating severe difficulties. Since the underlying difficulties cannot be spirited away by avoiding price variations in the exchange markets, they erupt in other forms, from changes of interest rates to direct interference with international trade and payments.

The important relationship between exchange-rate and interest-rate variations deserves a brief comment. We must remember that, under the gold mechanism, market economies had to pay for their fixed parities by being forced into artificially changing another price of strategic importance, namely, the short-term rate of interest. In simulating international price stability of the national monetary unit, the national monetary authorities were forced to change the domestic cost of borrowing money. From the standpoint of the principles of a market economy, this was a doubtful practice. Exchange-rate fluctuations, had they been permitted, would have been the automatic and instant result of changing supply and demand conditions in the foreign-exchange markets. Fixed par values, on the other hand, forced the market economies to transfer the adjustment function from the exchange rate to the interest rate, that is, from where it would have been natural to where it had to be induced artificially. Flexible exchange rates would have affected only international transactions; changes in interest rates had to affect the entire economy. Furthermore, while floating exchange rates would have been an equilibrating device in and by themselves, the discount rate affected international economic transactions only indirectly and belatedly through changes in national price levels.

It cannot be denied, of course, that exchange-rate variations imply some risk. However, it is not at all clear why, in a market economy, in which practically all transactions are connected with some risk, foreign traders should be especially protected and actually subsidized by their governments through the maintenance of fixed par values. Moreover, exchange risks can be transformed into known costs by the process of hedging, in which foreign currency is being bought at a given price for future delivery, the risk being borne by the speculator.

We have already seen that, far from being the cause of dangerous uncertainties, flexible exchange rates may, on the contrary, protect the economy against economic disturbances from without, such as imported inflation or unfair competition via competitive undervaluation.

Recent experiences with floating exchange rates have shown that floating does not have to lead to wild gyrations, not even in the wake of international monetary crises which were produced by an unfortunate combination of the par-value system with the dollar standard.

6

The Gliding Band and Managed Floating

Approaches to Greater Flexibility of Exchange Rates

The executive directors of the International Monetary Fund have recently indicated that they are willing to consider some new proposals for greater, but still limited, flexibility of exchange rates: first, a slight widening of the band for permissible exchange-rate variations; second, changes of par values without concurrence of the Fund, as long as such changes do not exceed 3 percent per year; and third, temporary deviations from par-value obligations, that is, the introduction of floating exchange rates under proper safeguards and for limited periods only.[1]

Three other "regimes," however, are excluded by the executive directors as "inconsistent with the par-value system." They are: freely floating exchange rates; substantially wider margins; and various systems in which the par value would change frequently according to objective indicators.[2]

The majority of a group of experts (consisting of officials from banking and business firms and economists) that had been reviewing similar proposals in 1969 in Bürgenstock, Switzerland, came to the conclusion that changes in exchange rates "when appropriate should take place sooner and, thus, be generally smaller and more frequent, than during the past two decades." [3] The majority favored "both widening the range (or 'band') within which exchange rates may respond to market forces, and permitting a more continuous and gradual adjustment of parities." The Bürgenstock Communiqué of 1969 and the Report of the Executive Directors of 1970 both indicate that proposals for greater flexibility of exchange rates may well become the core of international monetary reform.

Since the Fund authorities continue to stress the par-value system, it is advisable to concentrate first on the widened band and the gliding or "crawling" parity, preferably in the form of a combination of the two, the gliding or crawling bank. However, very recent experiences with managed floating have been reasonably successful, and should by now have removed the worst fears about floating. It is conceivable, therefore, that greater flexibility of exchange rates will not be approached from the par-value end of the spectrum of possibilities, but from these recent experiences with floating. The problem would then be to develop generally acceptable criteria for managed floating. We may assume, however, that the two approaches, the gliding band and managed floating, will turn out to be very much alike.

The Gliding Band

Before studying the gliding band, we should first try to find out what a substantial widening of the band alone might be able to do for the adjustment process. It could be argued that a much wider band of, say, 15 percent might permit maintenance of external equilibrium without requiring any par-value adjustments. This regime could perhaps be recommended on the ground that it would combine sufficient leeway for exchange-rate variations with the discipline claimed for unalterably fixed parities, an attractive combination, provided that divergencies between national monetary policies could be kept within the range permitted by the system's flexibility. It is not impossible that, with such a system, we could have avoided most adjustments of major currencies within the last twenty-five years, owing to the instant effect that realistic exchange rates would have had on resource allocation.[4]

More promising than a combination of a substantially widened band with permanently fixed par values, however, might be a system in which moderate margins of, say, 3 percent on either side of par (or a band of 6 percent) were attached to parities that are neither permanently fixed nor subject to major adjustments under conditions of fundamental disequilibrium. Rather, the par values would be permitted to change very frequently and in very small amounts whenever they would be in danger of moving away from realistic levels. In other words, the band would glide or crawl with the parity.[5]

The proposal for a gliding parity can be interpreted as a return to the adjustment mechanism of the Keynesian Clearing Union. We remember that this mechanism was to rest on relatively frequent par-value changes, whenever the members' debits and credits with the Union exceeded predetermined levels. The difference between a gliding parity and Keynes's proposition lies mainly in the fact that the recent plans want to divide parity adjustments into still smaller installments, with the aim of avoiding disequilibrating speculation.

In the following discussion of the gliding band it is assumed that a band of, say, 6 percent is moved up or down frequently as the centers of the band, the par values, are shifted. However, the par values themselves would not be permitted to change by more than, say, 3 percent for any twelve-month period, and correspondingly smaller percentages for shorter periods.

This combination of exchange-rate variations within a broadened band with small but frequent parity adjustments would have the following advantages.

1. Compared with a moderate widening of the band, the gliding band would permit parity adjustments whenever exchange rates get stuck at the upper or lower limit of the band.

2. Compared with a substantial widening of the band, a narrower band around a gliding parity would give assurance that exchange-rate fluctuations will be kept within relatively narrow limits over the short run.

3. Compared with a wide band in a system with permanently fixed parities, the gliding band would have the advantage of being open-ended. If the monetary policy of a member diverged continuously from the average behavior of the other countries in the same direction, the parity could change, the extent of the adjustment being limited, however, both for the short and the longer run.

4. Compared with the Bretton Woods system of the adjustable peg, the gliding band would maintain realistic exchange rates through frequent parity changes and fluctuations within the band. It would avoid the building-up of payments crises which are the result of unduly delayed par-value adjustments.

5. Compared with rare and large parity changes, the small adjustments implied in the operation of the gliding band would raise fewer political difficulties. "There would be less outcry from domestic pressure groups. Exchange rates would become less newsworthy, less likely to arouse irrational nationalistic reactions, and more easily subject to informed political debate." [6]

Since the executive directors of the Fund have indicated their willingness to consider both a slight widening of the band and an amendment to the Articles of Agreement that would "allow members to make changes in their parities without the concurrence of the Fund as long as such changes did not exceed, say, 3 percent in any twelve-month period nor a cumulative amount of, say, 10 percent in any five-year period," [7] we may hope that international monetary discussions will be able to work out the details of an improved adjustment process via greater, but still limited, flexibility of exchange rates, unless an alternative system of managed floating can be established.

The Gliding Band and Capital Movements

When the rejection of permanently fixed parities and freely floating exchange rates leads us to a system with greater, but still limited, flexibility of exchange rates, we have a system in which variations of exchange rates are to some extent substituted for changes in interest rates as they are used, for instance, under the gold-standard mechanism.

In normal cases, the widening of the band will induce equilibrating capital movements. A deficit country with full employment will raise its interest rates in an effort to halt inflation. It will then experience an inflow of foreign capital, not only because of the higher rate of interest, but also because speculators will buy the depreciating currency in expectation of a rebound, that is, a future appreciation. The inflow of capital allows the deficit country time for adjustment; it may even remove the need for adjustment in real terms, that is, in terms of a reallocation of productive resources, if the external disequilibrium should turn out to be only temporary. Changes of the parity will then be unnecessary. The widened band alone will furnish the needed flexibility. In essence, this is still the case of slightly widened margins between gold points.

More problematic is the dilemma case in which the surplus country S enjoys full employment while the deficit country D suffers from unemployment. This situation could, for instance, be the result of wage increases in D that exceed the increase in labor productivity. S raises the rate of interest in an attempt to stem price inflation, while D lowers its interest rate to stimulate economic activity. We have already seen that, when the exchange rate is unalterably fixed within very narrow limits, capital will flow from D to S, thereby increasing inflationary pressures in S and reducing employment still further in D. External disequilibrium deteriorates further in both countries.

In the Bretton Woods system of the adjustable peg, we produce disequilibrating international capital movements that are even worse than those to be expected in a system with unalterable parities. The more evident it becomes that D-currency will have to be devalued and S-currency upvalued, the more tempting it will be to shift capital from D to S. A system with a widened band in which the exchange rates would get permanently stuck at the support points would be exposed to the same criticism. The elasticity of the system would not be capable of absorbing the discrepancies in the members' monetary policies.

What would be the effect of a gliding-band system on interest rates and capital movements? Other things remaining equal, it would seem that with a downward crawl of the parity by 2 percent per year, capital would tend to flow out of the deficit country to avoid losses from depreciation, unless the country raised its interest rate by approximately the same amount. Similarly, an upvaluation of the surplus currency by 2 percent per year would have to be compensated by lowering the rate of interest correspondingly to prevent an unwanted influx of foreign capital.

This method of dealing with disequilibrating foreign funds through interest-rate differentials seems to take away the main advantage of greater flexibility of exchange rates, namely, the greater freedom that the gliding band is supposed to allow for domestic economic policies. The following points must be considered, however.

1. Disequilibrating capital movements would, in any case, be much less of a problem under a gliding-band regime than under the adjustable-peg system. The latter encourages substantial undervaluations and overvaluations whose eventual correction can be anticipated by private speculation. The former, the gliding-band system, would use frequent but small parity changes which would not induce disequilibrating flows of capital of the size with which the par-value system had to cope in the recent past.

2. The need to raise interest rates need not be detrimental to the domestic economy. The depreciating deficit country suffers, as a rule, from a higher-than-average rate of inflation. Therefore, a price inflation of, say, 2 percent would, in effect, cancel a 2 percent increase in rates of interest. The *real* rate of interest would remain the same, since the higher rate would simply compensate for increased commodity prices.

3. The gliding-band regime would try to emphasize symmetry in parity adjustments between deficit and surplus countries. Surplus countries would be expected to compensate for an upward crawl of their par values by a lowering of their short-term rates of interest, to prevent an undesirable influx of capital. The deficit countries then need no longer bear the full brunt of the adjustment.

4. A country's parity would not always crawl in one direction only. If the gliding band succeeds in building an adjustment mechanism into the international-payments system, we can expect reversals in the deficit or surplus positions of the participating countries. Speculators then can no longer be sure which way the market will turn in the longer run and disequilibrating capital movements will be reduced.

5. The combination of a widened band with very small parity changes will have the great advantage of making for very smooth par-value adjustments. As a matter of fact, a parity change need not even alter the existing market rate of exchange, since the latter may find itself still within the band around the *new* parity.

Operational Questions

The introduction of a gliding band poses the question whether, within the limits of the band, exchange rates are to be free to respond to market forces or are to be under the management of the national monetary authorities.

Within the widened band, the monetary authorities could leave the determination of the exchange rate entirely to market forces, intervening through buying and selling operations only at the margins. Alternatively, the authorities could try to influence the exchange rates inside the band in their desire to maintain "orderly" market conditions. A third possibility would be an "inner" band in which the authorities would promise not to intervene, while the outer fringes of the band would be permissible terrain for transactions by monetary authorities.[8]

Intervention inside the band can be justified with the argument that it would give a valuable tool to central banks. Occasions might arise in which a simultaneous fine-tuning of interest rates and exchange rates could produce desirable results; and, in practice, it will probably be impossible anyhow to get the consent of central bankers to the introduction of a gliding-band arrangement unless official market intervention is permitted.

The argument against such market intervention is twofold. First, the band is widened for the very purpose of giving market forces a better chance to make themselves felt. Variations inside the band will be an important indicator in connection with par-value adjustments. An authority that keeps the exchange rate from reacting to genuine market forces deprives itself of the most basic of all guidelines. Second, official interventions may be used to prevent the correct valuation of the currency in question, with the intention of gaining an unfair competitive advantage. A surplus country's monetary authority may purchase all foreign exchange that cannot be sold to private parties, and thereby prevent an appreciation or upvaluation of its currency.

The asymmetrical working of the par-value system has led to proposals for countervailing arrangements in a gliding-band regime.[9] These proposals urge that variations of exchange rates and parity adjustments should, in the main, be appreciations and upvaluations rather than, as in the past, predominantly movements in the opposite direction. This argument for a built-in counterweight against asymmetry emphasizes the stronger economic position of surplus countries, the unfair competitive advantage of undervaluation, imported inflation, and the danger implied in the preponderance of devaluations for the competitive position of the United States. It has been proposed that asymmetrical margins be established (for instance, a 1 percent margin for depreciation and a 3 percent margin for appreciation) and that the range of parity adjustments per period of time should be more generous in the upward direction.

Such proposals will face strong opposition. The surplus countries, in particular, will argue "that appreciation of the surplus countries' currencies instead of depreciation of the deficit country's currency . . . would be tantamount to imposing a painful cure on the healthy rather than on the sick." [10] Since an asymmetrical gliding band would imply stricter limits on downward adjustments, we can expect that it would also be rejected by deficit countries.

In the attempt to ensure correct behavior of member countries in connection with the operation of a gliding-band system, a careful surveillance of changes in the members' international liquidity reserves by the International Monetary Fund could play a major role. Where exchange-rate variations are interfered with, and unrealistic parities maintained, fluctuations in international liquidity reserves will betray misdemeanor. Surveillance of reserves, therefore, can be used to prevent violations.

Since governments are not likely to bind themselves to automatic parity adjustments, and since the executive directors of the Fund have already rejected proposals to effect parity changes on the basis of objective indicators, it may be advisable to follow the suggestion of Richard N. Cooper that we lay down presumptive rules "which no country is obliged to follow, but which each country could be expected to follow in the absence of sound and persuasive reasons for not doing so." Changes in parities would be keyed to changes in liquidity reserves "relative to some normal, desired reserve increase." [11]

Transition Problems

It is important that adjustment through a gliding band should not be expected to solve the task of clearing away all the debris which the par-value system has left in its wake. The par values should first be realigned, possibly during a period during which members, and particularly members with surplus positions, let their exchange rates float. The introduction of a wider band in December 1971 has often been misunderstood as a measure designed to correct mistakes in realigning the parities. This attitude is wrong, since the widening was very modest (from 2 to 4½ percent) and not accompanied by the gliding parity. We cannot expect much of so small a band around unrealistic par values. The exchange rates will immediately get stuck once more at the support points.

It would be wrong, on the other hand, to provide for broad bands and substantial "crawls" for transition purposes. The gliding band is to be the adjustment mechanism for the more normal situation in which the effects of diverging national economic policies are corrected and absorbed by small adjustments, so that fundamental disequilibria will no longer develop.

Assuming that we can start with realistic par values, it has been proposed that we could introduce a gliding band in stages, starting with a modest broadening of the band and a very limited range for the crawl, and then permitting more liberal ranges as the operators of the system gain in experience and courage. This gradualism looks attractive but is exposed to the danger that small values for band and crawl may not suffice to compensate for potential discrepancies between national monetary policies. In that case the system may be judged unworkable before it has been given a fair chance.

The gliding band would improve the international monetary system even if we should not succeed in eliminating the dollar standard. If the gliding band would work better and more symmetrically than the adjustable-peg system, the competitive position of the United States would be improved. Even if the dollar could fluctuate only indirectly via the changes of other parities, the reduced surplus of others would cut the deficit of the United States, and the remaining deficit would still be financed by automatic dollar purchases in the surplus countries. The introduction of the gliding band, therefore, can be considered independently from the role which the dollar plays in the system.

The Bürgenstock Communiqué, in recommending a wider band and more continuous and gradual adjustments of parities, stressed "that such innovation should be so framed as to facilitate continued international economic cooperation, while leaving individual countries or groups of countries free to adopt their own approach to their own individual circumstances." [12] As Harry G. Johnson has pointed out, even under a system with a gliding band "most countries would probably peg their currencies to our or another major currency, so that much international trade and investment would in fact be conducted under fixed rate conditions, and uncertainty would attach only to changes in the exchange rates among a few major currencies or currency blocs." [13]

Managed Floating

The proposal for a gliding band rests on the assumption that the members of the International Monetary Fund will reestablish par values for their currencies and adjust them much more frequently thereafter. Eventual return to par values is still the official line of the Fund. However, the widespread recourse to floating, and its remarkable success, make it seem possible that the proposal for a gliding band will have to compete with suggestions for a system with an elaborate management of floating. The difference between the two regimes may seem great when we consider that they approach a solution of the international-payments problem from opposite sides, as it were; it may seem only minor if we remember that managed floating means permanent market interventions, and that the gliding band implies the prevention of market fluctuations that exceed certain stated limits. One proposal is the mirror image of the other. Fritz Machlup is correct:

In principle, it would be possible to operate a system of managed floating that is *de facto* equivalent to a system of gliding parities. This may sound paradoxical in as much as floating currencies have no par values. However, central values or central intervention rates may take over the role that parities have under a crawling-peg system. Instead of altering the official parities with strict limits regarding the size of each single change and the size of the cumulative change over each twelve-month period, one may manage the floating in precisely the same way, observing the same limits for alterations of intervention rates. From a strictly economic point of view there need not be any difference between the two systems. There may, however, be strategic differences in the credibility of the two systems and in the possibility of obtaining guarantees of financial support from an international body such as the I.M.F.[14]

The fact that the floating of major currencies has recently been successful and has prevented the recurrence of international monetary crises should help remove exaggerated fears that so far have characterized the discussion of floating—fears of wild fluctuations of exchange rates, of competitive exchange depreciation, of disequilibrating speculation, of lack of monetary discipline, and of rampant world inflation.

Of course, managed floating is not going to stop world inflation. However, the adjustable-peg system was not able to do that either, and floating enables surplus countries to defend their more conservative monetary policies against imported inflation, and is, in this sense, rather an anti-inflation weapon.

The prejudice still persists that floating is more or less identical with competitive exchange depreciation. Advocates see it, on the contrary, as a guarantee of greater symmetry and avoidance of competitive undervaluation which plagued the Bretton Woods system.

To be sure, recent floating has not been free or pure. Monetary authorities have in some cases interfered through payments controls, and in practically all cases intervened by buying and selling operations to maintain "orderly" market conditions. Ideally, these "smoothing" operations should be designed to avoid only day-to-day fluctuations. Adjustments, even over the very short run, should not be prevented. Interventions should always be modest and limited to very short periods of time. These limitations are implied in the concept of floating. Managed floating with the aim of maintaining long-run stability of exchange rates would be self-contradicting.

If managed floating were used to maintain undervalued exchange rates for competitive advantages or overvalued rates for political reasons, these policies would reveal themselves in the form of growing or falling liquidity reserves. To maintain a low value for the local currency in the face of increasing foreign demand, foreign currencies would have to be absorbed through official purchases. Such a policy of competitive depreciation or undervaluation would have the consequence of imported inflation and give wrong price signals. It would negate the very purpose of floating. A policy of overvaluation via managed floating would have to be based on the official sale of foreign exchange out of reserves. Such sales could not continue for long, however. This shows that a system with managed floating is more likely to be misused by surplus than by deficit countries, and is in need of international supervision.

These considerations strongly recommend a "fixed reserve" standard, as proposed by Donald B. Marsh on the basis of Canadian experiences.[15] Par values would be replaced by floating exchange rates, with the proviso, however, that official reserves are permitted to fluctuate only within a pre-determined "reserve band." Obviously, Marsh's proposal refers to managed rather than free floating, since in the latter liquidity reserves would be superfluous.

Rules about fluctuations or variations of reserves need not determine the average size of the liquid assets a country likes to maintain, provided only that they neither grow above nor fall below a given original level by more than a predetermined amount. But obviously, large reserves, in-herited from the past, would then become unnecessary and uneconomical. With an effectively reduced international liquidity preference in all countries, excessive reserves should be channeled into long-term foreign invest-ment.

A comparison of managed floating with a gliding-band arrangement shows that they differ only in technical detail. Both want very small and very frequent changes of exchange rates as means of international payments adjustment; both want to permit national economic policies to follow policies of their own choosing without interference from the outside; and both want to bring about adjustment by a method that fits the rules of the market economy.

Seen politically, the systems differ. Advocates of the gliding band may claim the advantage that it can be interpreted as an improved way of operating the old par-value system; advocates of managed floating, on the other hand, can refer to the recent success of the system, and maintain that it would be logical to refine its management techniques.

The gliding band sets predetermined limits for variations of exchange rates; managed floating must refer to changes in reserve assets, which may be difficult to ascertain. The gliding band may sometimes prove to be still too rigid considering possible deviations of national monetary policies which may exceed the adjustment capability of the gliding band. Managed floating, on the other hand, removes in the eyes of some observers that critical "point of reference" (the par value) without which the national monetary authorities are supposed to be in danger of becoming entirely irresponsible.

Both systems must beware of the danger that proved to be the undoing of the Bretton Woods regime—the tendency of national monetary authori-ties to engage in overambitious smoothing operations. The greater the fear of "premature" changes of exchange rates, the greater will be the deviations from realistic rates and the inducement of disequilibrating capital movements. The latter, then, will make the authorities probably even more eager to intervene in the exchange market to prove that their wrongly chosen rates were correct. As Milton Friedman puts it:

Having made a mistake, there will be a strong resistance to recognizing it, a strong tendency to hang on and hope that circumstances will change and show that it was not a mistake, a strong tendency to convert what might have been a minor exchange rate movement into a major disequilibrium and crisis.[16]

In both systems, the gliding band and managed floating, it may be necessary to make a virtue rather than a sin out of small changes of exchange rates, since habits inherited from the Bretton Woods system tend strongly to undue delays. Errors in judgment would not matter too much, provided that the changes are very small and very frequent.

7

Which Standard: Gold, Dollar, or SDR?

Gold, SDRs, and Dollars

The main contenders for the role of international reserve asset and international unit of account are gold, the U.S. dollar, and SDRs. The trend seems to be in the direction of a gradual demonetization of gold, while the dollar faces a reduction in its international role. The factors determining our ultimate choice are political rather than economic. Each alternative solution has different advantages and disadvantages for the participating countries. The result will be a political compromise rather than an optimal economic solution. It is probable that we shall reconstruct the international monetary system not all at once but in installments with the emergence of the SDR as unit of account and main reserve asset.

International liquidity could be suddenly and dramatically increased by a general upvaluation of gold in terms of all national currencies. The official price of gold, for instance, could be doubled or tripled. Like the creation of SDRs, this measure would create international liquidity without creating a corresponding debt. Unlike the SDRs, however, gold reserves have, in the eyes of many observers, the enormous advantage of intrinsic value. By contrast, SDRs are the product of international agreement, and therefore subject "to uncertainty inherent in the nature of agreements between sovereign states." [1] Gold reserves have the psychological advantage of a fall-back value as commodity. SDRs seem to be in need of a gold guarantee that puts gold into the role of the ultimate standard good. We have to ask, therefore, whether liquidity creation via the upvaluation of gold might not be better than SDR creation. Gold seems to be able to solve the liquidity and confidence problem, and some advocates of gold still believe that it could solve the adjustment problem too, if only we were willing to return to a modernized gold-standard mechanism after a general upvaluation of gold.

The purchasing power of gold in terms of commodities was always determined by the average of permissible national credit expansion on the basis of given gold reserves. After World War II, the value of gold was for a long time determined by the purchasing power of the U.S. dollar; and today it has become unthinkable that changes in gold reserves would dictate monetary policy in the United States or in any other country. The abolition

69

of gold-backing requirements for national currencies was an acknowledgment of the creeping demonetization of gold in the national economies, and suggests that international demonitization of gold may be the logical sequel.

Gold and the U.S. dollar have served together as the unit of account of the Bretton Woods system. However, the development of the dollar glut, plus the growing danger of inconvertibility of the dollar into gold, made gold an object of disequilibrating speculation, rather than the pivot around which the international-payments system was safely turning.

In 1961, when it became too much for the United States alone to intervene in the gold market to maintain the dollar's gold parity, a gold pool of seven members helped meet the private demand for gold at the official par value. These common gold-market interventions ceased in March 1968, when the gold pool stopped supplying the private demand and buying newly mined gold for monetary reserve purposes. The present so-called two-tier system was established. Two separate markets for gold, an official and a private one, meant two separate prices: a fixed official par value, applying to transactions between central banks, and a private market price of gold, which was now permitted to deviate permanently from the official gold parity. While it lasts, this two-tier system must be interpreted as a further step toward the international demonetization of gold. Since 1968, gold no longer supplies additional international liquidity reserves.

Before August 15, 1971—that is, before the end of dollar convertibility into gold (or "the closing of the gold window")—gold still seemed to play a role as ultimate backing behind official dollar balances of foreign countries. The members of the gold-dollar system maintained their parities with the dollar by using the dollar as intervention currency; and the United States, in turn, stood supposedly ready to convert official foreign dollar balances on demand into gold. Gold convertibility of the dollar was seen as "the only means that others have to express dissatisfaction with dollar hegemony." [2] In fact, however, the United States was not put under serious political pressure. As the net-reserve position of the United States deteriorated, most member countries decided to refrain from asking for the impossible, namely, the conversion of a large and growing amount of dollar balances into a smaller and falling amount of gold. With the exception of de Gaulle, nobody wanted to wreck the system by putting the United States to the gold-conversion test.

The tying-together of gold and the U.S. dollar ("as of July 1, 1944") in the Bretton Woods system and the insufficiency of the Fund's resources had the practical result that foreign-held dollar balances gradually replaced gold as the world's most important liquid asset. Dollar balances, as interest-bearing assets, were considered preferable to sterile gold. Furthermore, since the value of gold depended on the purchasing power of the dollar which was continuously decreasing, gold production became less and less profitable, and added little to the gold stock. Additional international liquidity depended increasingly on U.S. deficits.

With the benefit of hindsight, we can see several ways in which this building-up of a potentially dangerous situation could have been avoided. Not only could we have created a much stronger international monetary organization such as the Clearing Union, we could also have gradually increased the price of gold in terms of all national currencies. This would have upvalued the existing gold stock and increased the yearly supply of newly mined gold. Foreign-held dollar balances need not have grown so much; gold-convertibility of the dollar might not have been questioned; and, the Europeans like to argue, the United States would not have been tempted into unwise policies through her automatic borrowing rights.

As long as gold and dollar seemed firmly tied together and nobody expected a dollar devaluation, however, a *gradual* increase of the price of gold was never seriously considered, and by the time the weakness of the system became obvious, a *substantial* upvaluation of gold became a hot political issue rather than an easy economic remedy. Furthermore, even the advocates of a substantial increase of the price of gold could not agree on which problem the measure was supposed to solve.

The Upvaluation of Gold

Distinguishing the issues of liquidity, adjustment, and confidence, we can discern a corresponding grouping among the advocates of an upvaluation of gold. Economists like Roy Harrod or Peter Oppenheimer [3] request a general upvaluation of gold as a drastic measure to increase world liquidity. The general raising of the price of gold would instantly create much larger reserves and increased freedom for domestic economic policies. But other advocates of a general upvaluation of gold are of the opposite opinion that liquidity creation under the gold-dollar standard has already been far too liberal, if not downright automatic. Jacques Rueff and Michael A. Heilperin, [4] for instance, feel that foreign-held dollar balances ought to be replaced by gold reserves. To make this replacement technically possible, however, it is inevitable first to increase the value of the existing gold stock and to stimulate gold production. When international liquidity reserves consist of gold alone, changes in gold reserves could be used once again to integrate national economic policies. Finally, authors like Milton Gilbert and Don D. Humphrey [5] propose a general revaluation of gold as precondition for an improved net-reserve position of the dollar and as means by which confidence in a gold-dollar system could be strengthened.

A general upvaluation of gold, such as a doubling or tripling of its price in terms of all currencies, must be criticized on the following grounds.

1. A general upvaluation of gold would favor countries that are either gold producers or happen to have large gold reserves. The additional liquidity would tend to go to countries that need it least. Politically speaking, not only would South Africa and Russia gain but also nations which, like France, have hoarded gold and contributed little to the effectiveness of the present international-payments systems.

2. A mere upvaluation of gold would increase world reserves, but would do nothing to correct their existing maldistribution.

3. Future international liquidity would be supplied in the most expensive form, namely through gold production, rather than through the creation of SDRs or similar instruments which can be supplied without production costs.

4. A sudden major increase in the value of gold reserves, unless counterbalanced by gold-sterilization policies, would strengthen the existing trend toward worldwide inflation.

5. The upvaluation of gold would have to be repeated again and again. The advocates of a general upvaluation of gold see it, as a rule, as a one-time measure. The reason is obvious. If future upvaluations are anticipated, it will be impossible to keep gold from disappearing into hoards.

6. Some advocates assure us that repeated upvaluations would not be necessary because the stimulation of gold production would supply an adequate amount of gold reserves. The belief that the future supply of gold will be neither excessive nor deficient rests on the old argument that a falling-off of gold production would lead to a worldwide decline of commodity prices, to lower production costs of gold, and to increased profitability of gold mining; whereas an excessive supply of gold would lead to inflated prices, higher costs of gold production, and reduced profitability of gold mining. This argument, which was not justified even in the heydey of the gold standard, is today utterly unrealistic. With creeping inflation, the price of gold would again and again get out of line with the rest of commodity prices, and require repeated upward revisions to stimulate gold production and to supply sufficient gold reserves.

7. Of course, the inflationary impact of a given upvaluation of gold would be greater if the measure was meant as an addition to existing liquidity reserves than as a replacement for foreign-held dollar balances. In Harrod's plan, the upvaluation of gold would add to already existing inflationary fuel, worldwide inflation might accelerate, and the revaluation of gold would have to be repeated periodically. If we follow Rueff's plan, a much sterner regime would guide domestic monetary policies once the discipline of the gold standard is reestablished. Worldwide inflation would be halted. However, Rueff can promise a permanently fixed gold value only on the basis of outdated assumptions. Members of the international monetary system are no longer willing to have their domestic policies determined by variations in gold reserves.

8. Michael Heilperin realizes that conversion of foreign-held dollar balances into gold will take time. He distinguishes two phases. In Phase I, any further accumulation of foreign-held dollar balances would be halted, so that the United States would be compelled to get her international payments into balance or face continued losses of gold. In Phase II, the United States would convert into gold all short-term dollar obligations still held by foreigners. Heilperin's proposal poses serious problems, however. In his eagerness to discipline the United States, he is willing to end suddenly and radically the "automatic" financing of U.S. deficits, while other countries, if they had large gold holdings to begin with, would command even larger reserves after the upvaluation of gold and the conversion of dollar balances into gold. It must be feared that the sudden deflationary effect on the United States and the inflationary impact on other countries might administer a dangerous shock to the international-payments system and to the domestic economies of its members.

The arguments for a general and substantial upvaluation of gold and a return to a full gold standard are not convincing. Arrangements concerning gold would have to rest just as much on political agreement as accords concerning the U.S. dollar or SDRs. The case for gold rests on its history as monetary disciplinarian. Under modern conditions, however, it is no longer realistic to expect that national monetary authorities will let their policies be dictated by variations in gold reserves.

If changes in international liquidity reserves should be of importance, for instance, in the adjustment of par values, their influence can be exerted quite independent of the composition of these reserves.

With the coming reconstruction of the international monetary system and the greater emphasis on flexible exchange rates, gold will no longer be needed as the disciplinarian that integrates domestic monetary policies.

The Dollar Standard

In the discussions that preceded Bretton Woods, the question of a new international standard unit was debated. Both Keynes and White suggested a special name for the new kind of money that was to be used between central banks. Keynes's *bancor* and White's *unitas* would have been international money both as means of payment and as unit of account. All member currencies would have been expressed in *bancor* or *unitas*, while these units, in turn, would have been defined in terms of gold. The gold value of *bancor* or *unitas* could have been changed, however. Keynes did not consider gold as the backing of *bancor*. He worked gold into his plan for reasons of expediency. "In discussing the question of why it is advisable to retain a provision for gold," he argued, the main point is, of course, that no scheme that did not make such a provision would have the smallest chance of acceptance in America, which has gold reserves, or in the British Empire, which has gold production, or in Western Europe, which has gold reserves, or in the Argentine, which has gold reserves, or in Russia, which has gold production. In short, there is no option.[6]

The Bretton Woods Agreement failed to create a new international monetary unit. Article IV determined that "the par value of the currency of each member shall be expressed in terms of gold as common denominator or in terms of the United States dollar of the weight and fineness in effect of July 1, 1944." This definition of the international unit of account established a gold-dollar standard. The dollar was the unquestioned numéraire in which the parities of other currencies were expressed. However, as the dollar-glut situation developed and a devaluation of the dollar in terms of gold was no longer inconceivable, gold rather than the dollar was seen by some monetary authorities as the ultimate international reserve asset. Gold appeared as the item with the intrinsic value which seemed to impart its value to the dollar as long as gold convertibility of the dollar was maintained. This interpretation was wrong, however, since changes in gold reserves had long ceased to exert a disciplining control over the monetary policies of the United States.

When gold-convertibility of the dollar ended on August 15, 1971, the gold-dollar standard became a pure dollar standard. The international-payments system did not break down as had been predicted and the dollar continued to be used as intervention currency. However, the dollar can serve as international unit of account only under the condition that the United States is willing to refrain from active intervention in the foreign exchange markets. In a world of N national currencies there can only be $N - 1$ exchange rates. In the past, the United States was willing to play the passive role of the Nth country and suffered for it, as we saw, because the other members of the system were generally much more inclined to devalue than to upvalue. It is doubtful, therefore, whether the United States will be willing to let its currency continue in the passive role of an international unit of account, and it is equally questionable whether the rest of the free world would want to accept such an arrangement.

That other countries were still willing to accumulate dollar balances can be explained, first, by the fact that an alternative was not readily available; second, by continuation of the dollar's convertibility into other currencies ("market convertibility"); and third, by the desire of some surplus countries to continue the undervaluation of their currencies vis-à-vis the dollar.

Under these conditions we might well ask whether it may not be best to simply continue with the dollar standard until a completely reconstructed international monetary system can be substituted. Improvements over the present situation would be possible in several ways, for instance, through value guarantees for official foreign dollar balances, through symmetrical exchange-rate flexibility, and, most important, through the removal of the so-called dollar overhang.

Some American authors advocate the maintenance of the present dollar standard as a policy of "benign neglect" on the part of the United States. The term is not very fortunate in that "neglect" implies insufficient attention while "benign" suggests to many foreign observers arrogance rather than kindliness. Benign neglect would mean, first, that, from the standpoint of the United States, national economic policies should be guided exclusively by domestic objectives, and second, that the initiative to change parities should be left entirely to other countries, the United States being willing to follow the completely passive role of the Nth country with respect to exchange-rate adjustments.

The proponents of a policy of benign neglect are eager to assert that it would not impose any hardships on other countries. Gottfried Haberler argues that

countries other than the U.S., when in persistent deficit which they can no longer finance by depleting reserves or by *ad hoc* borrowing, should promptly depreciate their currencies or, better, let them float. Countries in persistent surplus, if they do not wish to add to their reserves or let prices go up, should promptly appreciate their currencies, or, better, let them float up.[7]

It is true that under a much improved adjustment process via greater flexibility the pure dollar standard might work better than the gold-dollar standard under the adjustable-peg system. But experience has shown that countries are reluctant to promote domestic inflation (that is, "let prices go up") or harm their export industries by appreciation or upvaluation. Therefore, before an improved adjustment mechanism in the form of managed floating or a gliding band has proved its practicability, opinions will differ sharply on the desirability of a dollar standard. The surplus countries, at least, will continue to reject the suggestion that they inflate or appreciate in consequence of unilateral actions of the United States.

From the latter's standpoint, the benign-neglect proposal can be criticized with the argument that the United States should be permitted to participate equally in the adjustment of parities or the floating of exchange rates, and should not be forced to have the value of the dollar determined passively by the combined policies of all other countries. The United States could rely on these policies only if flexible rates could be made to work symmetrically. At present, the chances still are that devaluations and depreciations will tend to exceed upvaluations and appreciations, for the obvious reason that the deficit countries are forced to act when they run out of reserves, while surplus countries can accumulate reserves at will if they want to maintain a competitive undervaluation of their currencies. An excess of devaluations over upvaluations would mean that the dollar, as standard, would still tend to be overvalued to the competitive disadvantage of the United States.

As far as appreciations and depreciations inside a wider band are concerned, maintenance of the dollar standard would mean that the United States could enjoy only one-half of the leeway permitted to all other countries. Assume, for instance, that countries A and B find themselves at opposite margins of a band of 4½ percent, and that afterwards their positions are reversed completely. Their rates will now differ by 9 percent from the original position. Yet the dollar, as numéraire, could never move by more than 4½ percent in terms of any other currency!

Against these disadvantages could be held the fact that the United States could continue to borrow "automatically" as long as the rest of the free world is willing to maintain the dollar standard. Should further dollar devaluations become unavoidable, however, holders of dollar balances might incur losses in spite of the income from interest earned on these dollar balances. The possibility of losses could induce them to avoid further dollar accumulations. Even then the dollar standard might be maintained, however, provided the United States would be willing to extend a value guarantee to foreign official holders of dollar balances. A brief discussion of such guarantees may be in order, even though the chances are slim that they would be considered by the United States as the price for being permitted to play the dubious role of monetary leader in the free world. However, some form of guarantee would have to be used in any case should the International Monetary Fund be willing to exchange "Fund deposits" or SDRs for dollar balances in an effort to eliminate the dollar overhang. It is interesting to find out, therefore, what such value guarantees would imply.

Value guarantees have been used before to maintain confidence in the face of potential devaluation. We have seen that the Bretton Woods Agreement states in Article IV that "the gold value of the Fund's assets shall be maintained notwithstanding changes in the par or foreign exchange values of the currency of any member," and that, nearly a quarter of a century later, the special drawing rights were made subject to the same provision. The present uncertain position of gold, however, makes it necessary to look for another standard in which value guarantees can be expressed.

If the dollar were devalued in comparison with some standard unit, the United States could reimburse official foreign holders of dollar balances with additional dollars, so that the international purchasing power of their dollar reserves would stay the same. Such value guarantees would be difficult to introduce politically because they might involve many billions of dollars and could be considered unjust by domestic holders of savings accounts who do not enjoy a similar protection against loss of purchasing power through price inflation. Technically speaking, however, such guarantees would not involve insuperable difficulties for the United States as guarantor. The dollars to be added to foreign official accounts whenever the dollar is being devalued could be created by the Federal Reserve. No new taxes need be involved. The real question is what this would mean in economic terms. A cost-benefit analysis of value guarantees would have to consider the following points.

On the benefit side it is most important that the guarantor, in our case the United States, would gain the right to devalue within the framework of a dollar standard. Without this right the United States might have to pay with unemployment and slow growth for the willingness to let the dollar be used as international liquidity reserve. Another benefit would be the continuation of automatic borrowing rights which the United States would still enjoy.

The money costs involved, that is, the amount of additional dollars to be created, would depend on the size of the guaranteed foreign official balances and the rate of devaluation. The economic effect of huge creations of dollars for guarantee purposes could be inflationary for the United States if these dollars would be spent on U.S. exports. We might expect, however, that foreign central banks would want to hold on to these additional dollars so as to have, in terms of international purchasing power, the same reserves as before the dollar devaluation.

The most urgent problem concerning the dollar is the so-called dollar overhang. Tens of billions of official foreign dollar balances have been piling up as international reserve assets during the past twenty-five years. They pose a difficult problem which, unless solved, may block international monetary reform.

As long as the dollar was the most coveted international reserve asset, foreign-held dollar balances created no problem. With the coming of the dollar glut, the end of dollar convertibility into gold, and repeated dollar devaluations, enormous outstanding dollar balances have become a serious disequilibrating force whenever changes of major currencies are impending. These dollar assets can be likened to a loose cargo in a storm-tossed ship. International-payments crises, wherever they originate, tend to become dollar crises through the existence of the dollar overhang. To overcome these crises, therefore, we have to eliminate the dollar overhang.

An obvious solution suggests itself. If the members of the system are agreeable, all undesired dollar balances can be exchanged for specially issued SDRs or other liquid assets in the Fund ("Fund deposits"). The working-out of the details offers a wide range of choices. Attention would have to be given to the following points.

1. Considering that the members would deposit dollar reserves, the use of the substitute SDRs or Fund deposits would have to be completely unconditional.

2. The new assets would have to enjoy unquestioned confidence and

should be made better than the dollar balances they replace. This could be done if the Fund offered some kind of value guarantee plus appropriate interest payments. However, it is important also that the new assets be not made too attractive, because then the members would tend to hoard SDRs and use a substitute such as, for instance, newly acquired dollar balances.

3. The United States, in turn, would have to extend corresponding value and income guarantees to the Fund.

4. The dollars deposited with the Fund could not be expected to be "repurchased" by the United States with convertible currencies within a relatively short period. If the dollar standard were to be abolished, the United States could not afford to use all her payments surpluses for a reduction of her indebtedness to the Fund, since part of these surpluses would have the function to finance future deficits. The changeover from years of automatic borrowing to normal balance-of-payments behavior would be difficult enough without a huge extra burden in the form of enormous repurchase obligations.

5. It is not in the interest of other members of the system to put an excessive burden on the United States. Instead of saddling the world once more with a major transfer problem, it would be far better to consolidate the dollar overhang.

The SDR Standard

Effective July 1, 1974, exactly thirty years after the Bretton Woods Agreement, "the Fund has put into operation a new method of valuing the special drawing right (SDR) in terms of currencies, using the technique known as the 'standard basket'." Originally, the Fund valued SDRs in terms of dollars. "Exchange rates for SDR against other currencies were derived from representative market rates for those currencies against the dollar." This method of valuation was changed

following the declaration of the United States authorities in August 1971 that they would no longer convert foreign official dollar balances into primary reserve assets, and with the subsequent moves of Fund members to a system of widespread floating there was growing support for a different method of valuation.[8]

The sixteen currencies in the standard basket

are of those countries with a share in world exports of goods and services that averaged more than 1 percent in 1968–72. Relative weights for each currency are broadly proportionate to a country's exports, but are modified to recognize that the share in trade does not necessarily give an adequate measure of a currency's weight in the world economy.[9]

Individual currencies' exchange rates in terms of SDR are ascertained via their market rate in U.S. dollars together with the SDR-dollar rate. The Fund emphasizes that "this practice is . . . merely a question of convenience, and does not confer on the U.S. dollar any special status vis-à-vis the SDR."[10] However, we must remember with some concern that precisely the same situation was created when, thirty years ago, Article IV of the Fund Agreement stated that "the par value of each member shall be expressed in terms of gold as a common denominator or in terms of the United States dollar of the weight and fineness in effect July 1, 1944." The choice of the dollar as numéraire did, no doubt, contribute to the development of the dollar standard from which the SDR standard is now supposed to extricate us.

The standard basket technique is not much more than a statistical gimmick, since it is self-evident that the value of the SDR must be equivalent to the amount of the different currency units of the member countries that the SDR can buy. When we go one step further, we can see that the ultimate purchasing power of SDRs is established when we know not only the SDR values of the currencies but also the prices of the international traded commodities that can be bought with the currencies.

Ideally, we could aim at an SDR value that remains stable in terms of commodities. This aim of a permanently stable standard good has never been achieved, not even under the pre-1914 gold standard. However, it is conceivable that the members of the SDR system would always precisely adjust the SDR values of their currencies for changes in domestic price levels. Worldwide inflation, then, would express itself in a continuing appreciation of the SDR. Of course, the SDR yardstick would do nothing to prevent inflation.

It is most important that the *relative* SDR values of the member currencies be realistic. The standard basket value of the SDR could rise without harm to international monetary relations, provided that we keep the adjustment of the currencies' SDR values symmetrical.

Since the SDR has become the international unit of account, it seems only logical that the SDRs should become the main official reserve asset. Many practical proposals point in this direction, and it is not unlikely that a gradual transformation of other reserve assets into SDRs will become one of the two major aims of international monetary reform, the other being, of course, the improvement of the adjustment mechanism via greater flexibility of exchange rates.

Compared with the haphazardness of the supply of gold and U.S. dollars as international reserve assets, it is the virtue of SDR creation that reserves can be fed into the system by the conscious decision of an international agency. Potentially, we have here the instrument by the use of which the Fund can control the quantity of international money. In fact, however, SDRs are, for the time being, only a small part of the sum total of all international reserve assets. The assets outside the control of the Fund are still so large and volatile that the total supply of reserves cannot yet be determined by manipulating the creation of SDRs.

It would be relatively easy to regulate the total supply of international liquidity through SDR creation if the supply through all other sources combined could always be assumed to be insufficient relative to legitimate demand. SDR creation could then take care of the residual supply and be so managed as to make the total optimal. In reality, however, the new supply of reserve assets via, say, a deficit of the United States may be too large, even assuming a zero creation of SDRs for the period. If, therefore, SDR creation is eventually to lead to an orderly management of liquidity reserves, it is necessary that excess supplies of other reserve assets be somehow eliminated. The haphazardness of the supply of monetary gold reserves has already been tamed by the freezing of official gold reserves, and the dollar overhang can be eliminated if the members of the system are agreeable to accepting Fund deposits or SDRs in lieu of excessive dollar balances.

If the dollar standard were replaced by an SDR standard, it would seem that henceforth all official reserves would consist of (regular and) special drawing rights and that SDR creation (or the increasing of Fund quotas) would be the only source of additional international liquidity. However, there would also be a need for official working balances in national currencies. To maintain a given par value of its currency, a deficit country will have to sell foreign currencies to private buyers. These sales imply that central banks maintain working balances of national currencies. However, as long as such working balances are held, the danger exists that they may grow too much in connection with major deficits of key-currency countries. Assuming that interest rates on these balances are attractive enough, the trend toward a dollar (or any other key-currency) standard could be revived to the detriment of the SDR standard.

Tom de Vries suggests that a way to avoid this danger might be "an arrangement to the effect that each monetary authority would henceforth support the par value of its currency by buying and selling it on its exchange market for SDRs." But "such a system would make it necessary to allow private financial institutions to hold SDR balances, since they are the institutions with whom the monetary authorities deal on the exchange market." [11]

Still other changes in the present SDR arrangements would be necessary if we want to develop a full-fledged SDR standard. These changes would concern value guarantees and interest rates, the freedom of the use of SDRs, abolition of the reconstitution clause, and elimination of the rule that no participant is required to hold more than three times his own cumulative allocation of SDRs.

Successful development of an SDR standard could solve many of the problems connected with the present dollar standard. It would permit us to abolish the latter's one-sided advantages and disadvantages for the United States, and would be "making the world safe for a U.S. external equilibrium." [12]

8 The European Monetary Union

Optimum Currency Areas and Monetary Blocs

The present trend toward greater flexibility of exchange rates and more frequent adjustments of parities coincides with the decision of the members of the European Economic Community (EEC) to reach complete monetary union by 1980. At a minimum, this goal implies rigidly and permanently fixed parities between the EEC currencies; at a maximum, it may mean the creation of a European currency, for instance, a Eurofranc, with general acceptability throughout the area. In either case, monetary union would require complete integration of the monetary, fiscal, and wage policies of the participating countries.

Policies to achieve monetary union are the exact opposite of efforts to promote external balance through floating exchange rates or a gliding band. The latter try to give freedom to the members of the system to pursue their own domestic policy objectives. Monetary union eliminates, once and for all, any national divergence from a common regional course; it means the end of a national economic policy for the members.

However, the European Monetary Union will try to combine unalterably rigid parities *inside* the Union with greater flexibility toward the *outside,* in particular toward the U.S. dollar. The members of thet EEC feel that, for them, a common policy is both possible and advantageous for reasons that could not be applied on a worldwide scale. These reasons are partially political. As far as economics is concerned, they could have to do with the ease with which factors of production will supposedly move and the mutual interdependence of the countries of the region. If what is true for Europe applies also to other areas of the world, international monetary relations could become transactions between monetary blocs rather than between a multitude of independent nations. Each monetary bloc would consist of countries with closely integrated monetary policies and mutually fixed parities. The relationships between blocs, however, would be characterized by floating exchange rates or frequent adjustments of parities, simplified by the fact that only relatively few parities would be involved.

We see that an individual country need not make a clear-cut decision concerning the fixity or flexibility of its exchange rate. It can become a member of a monetary bloc and the bloc, in turn, can maintain flexible relationships with similar groupings. What a given country decides to do will depend on its geographical location and on its economic structure relative to that of its major trade partners. It may well be that it chooses to tie its exchange rate to that of another country. As Harry G. Johnson has pointed out, there are many small and relatively narrowly specialized countries, whose national currencies derive their usefulness "from their rigid convertibility at a fixed price into the currency of some major country with which the small country trades exclusively or on which it depends on capital for investment." [1] A fixed parity is more important in this case than greater scope for autonomous domestic policies via flexible exchange rates.

However, we deal here with a continuum. As we increase the size of the country and the diversification of its production, it will at some point become questionable whether it is still advisable to integrate its domestic economic policies with those of a *Leitwährungsland*. Flexibility of exchange rates might permit deviations of national monetary, tax, and wage policies and freedom for a country to disentangle itself from political and economic policies of its former leader that are considered mistaken or incompatible with the country's own economic aims.

Robert A. Mundell defines an "optimum currency area" as "an area within which exchange rates *ought* to be fixed." [2] He applies this concept consistently to cases in which an existing national unit such as the United States would have to be broken up into several more homogeneous sections with separate currencies. However, since the odds against the splitting-up of existing nation states into several optimum currency areas are overwhelming, the practical question can concern only the formation of currency blocs or monetary unions.

The argument for the formation of a monetary bloc can best be discussed with reference to the present effort to form a European Monetary Union, and by answering the question why this attempt to establish permanently rigid parities between the EEC currencies should be made at the very time when it has become obvious that the Bretton Woods system needs an improved adjustment mechanism through greater flexibility of exchange rates.

Arguments for a European Monetary Union

The political decision to create the Monetary Union was made shortly after the international monetary crisis of the fall of 1969, with the obvious intention to eliminate any future need for disturbing parity adjustments inside the EEC. Had French and German economic policies been adequately integrated, the crisis of 1969 would not have arisen. Accordingly it was argued that complete economic integration ought to be achieved between the EEC countries. This is the old belief that unalterably rigid parities can serve as disciplinarian, supported by the conviction that a regional cluster of interdependent countries could achieve a degree of economic cooperation that eludes the capacity of the free world as a whole. In the eyes of the advocates of a European Monetary Union, the members of the EEC constitute an optimum currency area, would gain, economically and politically, by complete integration, and, accordingly, should be willing to make whatever sacrifices are needed in terms of national sovereignty.

Devaluations (France) and upvaluations (Germany) inside the EEC have created major problems for the Common Agricultural Policy (CAP) of the EEC, which is based on a system of support prices for certain agricultural products. These support prices were expressed in a unit of account which had the same gold parity as the U.S. dollar of July 1944. This meant that an upvaluation of the German mark reduced German farm incomes. Farm receipts in dollar units could purchase only fewer marks than before. The French devaluation, on the other hand, meant that French farmers now received a higher income in terms of devalued French francs, since the support prices were fixed in "dollars." These conclusions, however, are not entirely correct. We do have to consider that if the French devaluation was primarily the result of excessive inflation in France, while the German upvaluation was due to Germany's more cautious monetary policy, the parity adjustments only put the farmers back into their original position in terms of purchasing power. This fact cannot prevent complaints, however, because of the shift of farm incomes compared with other income groups. The French farmer, for instance, was in the end protected against losses from inflation, while other Frenchmen were not. The German farmer, on the other hand, had the feeling of being injured, since the upvaluation made industrial products more expensive in terms of agricultural earnings. (These reactions, by the way, will add to the known asymmetry of parity adjustments, since the farm population in the EEC countries now feels that it has reason to favor devaluation and to oppose upvaluation.)

The reactions of the proponents of the European Agricultural Policy was predictably naïve. For the smooth functioning of the CAP it was simply necessary to make embarrassing parity adjustments impossible, that is, to establish a European Monetary Union. In fact, the supporters of the CAP had obviously taken a common monetary unit for granted because without it the CAP had to lead to explosive tensions.

Even if the economic costs of creating a European Currency Union were far greater than the economic benefits, it is still possible to argue that the *political* advantages of a common monetary policy would outweigh such disadvantages as increased inflationary pressure in Germany or growing unemployment in France. Unalterably rigid parities are seen as a precondition for political integration, communitywide legal instruments being seen as the *sine qua non* for making a common monetary policy workable.[3]

The interpretation of economic integration which stands behind this argument is too narrow, however, If we mean by international economic integration "a welding-together of national markets, so that potential buyers have an undiscriminated choice between home-made and imported goods," then we can achieve this kind of integration more easily with greater flexibility of exchange rates, undisturbed by "an institutional, organizational, not to say, bureaucratic, notion of what international integration means." [4]

Since the argument for permanently fixed parities is to apply only inside the EEC, flexibility can and should prevail in the EEC's relationship with other countries or monetary blocs. Freedom from the constraints under which Europe was placed by the de facto dollar standard was, obviously, one of the strongest arguments for the European Monetary Union. The arguments for greater flexibility of exchange rates are not rejected altogether, they are merely applied to the relations between the EEC and the United States. A common monetary policy for the EEC is seen as the way out of an unbearable situation in which the United States dominates the domestic monetary policies of the EEC countries whose central banks have to buy all the dollars left unsold at existing parities. The EEC countries "automatically" financed U.S. deficits resulting from policies (such as inflation, Vietnam, the "takeover" of industries inside the EEC) of which they disapproved not only on principle but also because they produced the phenomenon of "imported" inflation. The European Monetary Union, therefore, can be interpreted as the means for the EEC countries to leave the dollar standard without having to embark on a general system of managed floating.

Economic and Political Implications

To understand the implications of a monetary union the following points have to be considered.

1. Monetary union means full and permanent interconvertibility of the currencies of the member countries at permanently fixed exchange rates. It is absurd to speak of monetary union before the members have given up exchange controls over intraregional transactions.

2. More important in the long run is the fact that the members of the union have to surrender autonomy over their national monetary policy. Short-term rates of interest, for instance, cannot be permitted to vary significantly between members.

3. Since monetary and fiscal policies are closely interrelated, the members are left with very little freedom in terms of tax policies and public expenditures. In particular, inflationary deficit spending, as full-employment

policy, would be ruled out if it exceeded that of the other members of the union.

4. Still more far-reaching is the fact that a common monetary policy demands that wage rates in all participating countries be bound by the same monetary limitations. This does not mean, of course, that the wage level of the member countries would have to be the same. On the contrary, a common monetary policy implies that differences in labor productivity be matched by differences in wages in order to maintain interregional competitiveness at high employment levels.

5. As long as a monetary union is based on fixed parities rather than on a common currency, the "band" for permissible variations of exchange rates must be gradually reduced and finally abolished to achieve the equivalent of a common currency.

6. During its initial period a monetary union must establish some form of mutual assistance by which surplus members extend financial aid to deficit members. Obviously, such aid can only be temporary, limited, and conditional, lest it violate the logic of the effort toward full economic integration.

We have seen that the par-value system of Bretton Woods had to lead to repeated international monetary crises and to the growth of quantitative restrictions because the members of the Fund were not able to achieve sufficient economic integration. Yet this lack of integration was just as true for the EEC countries in relation to each other as for the rest of the Fund's members. Pressures created by diverging national monetary policies had to erupt in the form of major parity adjustments in Europe as much as in the rest of the world.

The economic case for a European Monetary Union rests on the proof that monetary integration can be achieved within the region without excessive cost, and on the demonstration that optimum resource allocation for the region could not be gained without fixed parities. The case for monetary union is weak on both counts.

It is extremely doubtful that monetary, fiscal, and wage policies of, say, France and Germany can be sufficiently integrated to make a monetary union workable. Suppose, realistically, that under a regime of permanently and rigidly fixed parities the French economy suffers a severe recession and that French unemployment exceeds what is considered tolerable both in France and in the EEC at large; assume further that, simultaneously, Germany's fully employed economy is exposed to inflationary pressure. Is it, then, likely that a common monetary policy for the union can be found that is equally acceptable to France and Germany? An expansionist policy that would increase employment in France would accentuate inflation in Germany, while a policy that would help stabilize German prices would possibly turn the French recession into a depression.

The obvious cure for this dilemma—an adjustment of par values—is ruled out once we assume the existence of a monetary union. France could no longer devalue the franc vis-à-vis the mark, Germany no longer upvalue the mark vis-à-vis the franc. The result would be growing political tensions which could by far exceed the difficulties that the parity adjustments of 1969 and after produced in connection with the Common Agricultural Policy.

Advocates of the European Monetary Union may want to suggest that, had the union been in existence, it would have prevented the very discrepancies behind our assumed tensions. But this would mean to argue that tensions are to be eliminated not by relieving pressure but rather by an even tighter squeeze through the elimination of the one safety-valve which the Bretton Woods experts built into the system, namely, the adjustment of parities.

Inherent Dangers

What will be the result of an irrevocable decision to establish a European Monetary Union if it later turns out that the members do not succeed in integrating their monetary, fiscal, and wage policies? First, probably, a weakening rather than a strengthening of political solidarity, owing to growing frictions in the vain struggle to achieve a common monetary policy; second, counterproductive effects in the national economies of the members such as, for instance, more inflation in Germany or more unemployment in France; third, further growth rather than elimination of quantitative restrictions in intraregional trade; and fourth, probably excessive liquidity creation to maintain parities in fundamentally unbalanced situations.

The result would be the regional counterpart of our worldwide experiences with the par value system, with the important difference, however, that the European Monetary Union would have abolished even the safety valve of parity adjustments in cases of fundamental disequilibria. The crisis that a monetary union could produce inside the European Economic Community, therefore, could be far worse than the monetary crises of the recent past.

John Maynard Keynes warned against England's return to the gold standard in 1925 as "a dangerous and unnecessary decision." [5] Nearly half a century later, the EEC authorities, too, must be criticized for having embarked on a dangerous and superfluous venture. Dangerous, because its consequences may create unbearable tensions in the fabric of the EEC, and unnecessary, because the desired regional integration—in the sense of a welding together of national markets—could be achieved with relative ease through frequent adjustments of parities when divergencies in national monetary, fiscal, and wage policies cannot be compromised.

In Europe's approach to monetary union the premise seems to be that political arrangements are to come first and that economic integration will follow. Realists feel that it would be far better to adjust the legal framework of the emerging union to the degree of economic integration that can actually be achieved. To them the political-pressure approach is a clear case of putting the cart before the horse.[6]

If we start with economic rather than with political integration, it makes sense to begin with greater flexibility of exchange rates instead of with reducing the width of the band, as was actually done in the EEC. If it turns out that the EEC countries can achieve a high degree of economic coordination among themselves, then it will not be necessary for them to make use of whatever kind of flexibility is built into the system. Exchange-rate variations inside the band and frequent parity adjustments would become less and less important. Alternatively, adequate flexibility with fixed parities could be provided by liberal financial arrangements through a common reserve pool, and these arrangements could become gradually less liberal as monetary integration proceeds and less financial assistance is needed. In any case, it would be wiser to find out experimentally how much flexibility is needed before a final commitment to unalterably fixed parities is made.

The political difficulties of complete monetary integration become evident when we try to answer the question as to which kind of common monetary standard the members of the union should choose. The standard might have to do with price stability expressed in a common unit of account. Each member, then, would have to see to it that its price level is kept in line with that of the bloc in general. However, in order to achieve this conformity, it would be indispensable to keep wages in line with the growth of productive efficiency in the individual member countries. As long as the nations forming the union face their problems with wage and cost-push inflations of different degrees, how can we expect their national authorities to sign away the safety valve of government deficit spending as the only way of avoiding mass unemployment, when labor unions insist on wage increases that exceed the rise in productive efficiency? In fact, monetary union might make it more difficult than ever to try to induce the labor leaders of the member countries to accept wage scales that correspond to labor productivity in their individual countries and industries. "Monetary union would enforce tendencies to equalize wage levels all through Europe, since cross comparison of nominal wages would become more easy than it is now."[7] The result might be either a regionwide "accommodating" inflation or, if the surplus members resist, a dissolution of the union under the pressure of conflicting interests.

The international monetary crises of 1973 have made it abundantly clear that Europe is not ready for monetary union.

At the end of 1972 the European Commission asked a group of economists to examine the possibilities and means of achieving economic and monetary union. The experts' report on *European Economic Integration and Monetary Unification*[8] points out that "a great gap exists . . . between official declarations of intent and concrete actions undertaken to further progress on economic integration and monetary unification." In the opinion of the experts, it is questionable that economic integration should be used as a lever to political integration. European Monetary Union can succeed only if simultaneous progress can be achieved over a wide area of monetary, economic, social, and political issues. For this reason, the experts emphasize "a new concept of parallelism." They want to say that monetary unification can only be achieved "if backed by a sufficient advance in economic integration to cope with conjunctural and structural imbalances, which monetary unification itself might even enhance."

Less-Developed Countries

The World Bank

Less-developed countries (LDCs) face special problems in the international relations, and since the larger number of the members of the International Monetary Fund belong into the LDC category, a study of international monetary reform must consider the particular international issues connected with economic development. Up to now, international monetary policy has mostly been formulated by the advanced industrial countries which, in the eyes of the less-developed countries, have not paid enough attention to the latter's special needs.

It is difficult to generalize about the economic problems of the LDCs, owing to great differences in their economic systems. Most of the developing countries have "mixed" economies. They do not operate under an all-inclusive central plan like the Soviet-type economies; yet, at the same time, they often do not have the benefit of a well-functioning market system either. Many of the emerging nations do not use the methods and instruments of a command economy which would overtax their administrative capabilities. On the other hand, competitive market forces are not held in high esteem either, because they have not made a very impressive showing in the past, as demonstrated by the underdeveloped state of their economies. Obviously, market forces lacked the right climate in which to operate and the support of essential government services. In addition, and above all, abject poverty in many of these countries keeps savings and investments low; and what little improvement in productive efficiency can be achieved is being outstripped by rapid population growth. Yet, as Gottfried Haberler has pointed out:

Many backward countries have adopted and are still in the process of initiating the latest policies which it took the advanced industrial countries decades or centuries to develop. The latest, most up-to-date legislation on social security, regulations of labor, minimum wages, working conditions, channeling saving through government agencies and impounding them for public purposes—all these policies which developed countries have adopted only in a late stage of their development are often introduced in underdeveloped countries as soon as they are freed from colonial status. Add equalization of income through progressive direct taxation, nationalization of existing enterprises and reservation for the Government of certain industries and you have an economic policy which greatly overtaxes the limited administrative capacities of underdeveloped countries.[1]

In external relations, too, the outlook is bleak. Depending as they often do on the capricious proceeds from the exports of primary products, the LDCs are sensitive to the economic health of industrial countries. In addition, domestic inflation, often combined with political reluctance to devalue, leads often to protracted overvaluations and corresponding shortages of international liquidity reserves.

The existence of special international economic problems of the LDCs was recognized at Bretton Woods but interpreted, in the main, as a huge demand for foreign long-term investment funds which, at least in the beginning, could not be met out of private sources alone. It seemed obvious, however, that the supply of long-term capital should not be entrusted to the International Monetary Fund, whose liquidity would be impaired if its resources were permanently tied down in investments goods production. Instead, a separate sister organization of the IMF was created, the International Bank for Reconstruction and Development (the so-called World Bank)—the clearest indication that international liquidity and investment problems were considered strictly separate issues.

In the beginning, the World Bank assumed that profitable investment opportunities abound in the LDCs, and that private foreign capital would be able to finance most of this demand. However, in its *Fourth Annual Report* for 1948–49 the IBRD was already ready to admit that "perhaps the most striking lesson which the Bank has learned in the course of its operations is how limited is the capacity of the underdeveloped countries to absorb capital quickly for really productive purposes." To achieve progress, it was first necessary to remove obstacles in the path of productive and profitable investment, such as inadequate education and training, poor health conditions, vested interests opposed to change, insufficient technical and administrative skills, lacking transport facilities, and many other impediments.

The special nature of the investment problem in LDCs made it necessary that careful consideration be given to appropriate investment priorities, a formidable task which involves nothing less than the drawing-up of a development program for the economy as a whole, with special emphasis on proper balance. However, in the absence of an all-inclusive central plan, this is an extremely difficult task in which little guidance can be expected from market forces. The basic investments that a poor country needs are to be found in the area of communal demand in which comparisons between interest rates and anticipated profits cannot be employed.

The World Bank has not yet succeeded in stimulating an adequate flow of private capital to the LDCs, the only flow, according to the *Fifth Annual*

Report of the IBRD, "that can provide external financial assistance in amounts sufficient to make a significant inroad on the world's development needs." The type of investment needed is often not profitable in the private-enterprise sense of the word, however productive it may prove to be in the long run. Furthermore, private capital in the developed industrial countries often does not want to accept the added risk of foreign investment when lucrative investment opportunities are plentiful at home. In going abroad, private capital faces the possibility of exchange controls that may prevent the transfer of profits or even expropriation by nationalization.

The World Bank has tried to meet such fears with its own guarantees and the requirement that, in the case of loans by the Bank to private enterprise, the member government in whose territory the investment project is located "fully guarantees the repayment of the principal and the payment of interest and other charges on the loan." [2] This well-intended guarantee, however, has done more harm than good because it has had the effect of discouraging private borrowers "who fear that a government guarantee might lead to interference by the government in the conduct of their business." [3]

Foreign borrowing creates future payments and transfer obligations. Loans must be serviced and repaid in foreign currency. This fact must be considered in the development plan. Investment of foreign capital must eventually lead to export surpluses that permit interest and amortization payments in convertible currencies.

The World Bank foresees cases of acute exchange stringency in which a borrowing member finds itself unable to live up to its promises. Should this happen, the member may apply for a relaxation of the conditions of repayment. The Bank may then (1) accept service payments in the currency of the member and arrange for the repurchase of such currency in the future, and/or (2) "modify the terms of amortization or extend the life of the loan or both." [4] Besides, the World Bank has created an affiliate institution, the International Development Association (IDA), which provides finance "on terms more flexible and bearing less heavily on the balance of payments of the recipient country than those of conventional loans." [5]

IMF and LDCs

The International Monetary Fund has left the problems of development finance to the World Bank. Only in connection with "compensatory financing of export fluctuations" has it taken the initiative. Recognizing that fluctuations in export proceeds had been much greater for primary producing countries than for others, the Fund authorities felt the need for adapting both the quotas and the drawing rights so that primary producers could maintain their import capability in spite of fluctuations in their income from exports. However, the drawings to meet the shortfalls were normally not to exceed 25 percent of a country's quota, and the shortfalls had to be attributable to circumstances beyond the member's control.

In spite of these endeavors, the reaction of the LDCs to the Fund's policies has not been too favorable. The Fund is often seen as a rich men's club, an institution dominated by a relatively small group of capitalist countries. Voting rights according to size of quota are considered unfair, and the tendency is strong to do what the experts at Breton Woods were determined not to do, that is, to make the Fund into a money-creating superbank for development financing.

This attitude is understandable when we consider the enormous differences in per-capita income between the poor and the rich countries together with the strong desire, particularly in socialist nations, to achieve a more equal income distribution not only domestically but internationally. Nevertheless, it would be dangerous to overlook the fact that the problems of development finance and of international payments, though occasionally overlapping, are basically different. Optimum creation of international liquidity (in the form of SDRs, for instance) cannot be determined by what the emerging nations can absorb to their advantage as long-term investment; nor would the sum total of international liquidity creation per annum be anywhere near large enough to satisfy the legitimate needs for foreign funds for development purposes.

At the same time it is understandable that the representatives of developing countries with urgent liquidity problems have little interest in monetary proposals coming from the rich nations, such as the suggestion of a general upvaluation of gold (which the poor do not have) or the allocation of SDRs to rich surplus countries (which do not need such extra reserves).

The issue of a "link" between liquidity creation (via SDRs) and development aid will play a decisive role in the reconstruction of the international monetary system. The poorer half of the members of the system will tend to argue for much more liquidity, particularly if liquidity can be had in the form of SDRs; and the richer half will tend to oppose excessive liquidity creation which, for them, means "imported" inflation.

Of course, not all rich countries are in the surplus nor all poor countries in the deficit category. As a matter of fact, surplus and deficit positions of the members of the system, rich and poor alike, should ideally speaking be subject to frequent reversals once a workable adjustment process via a gliding band or managed floating has successfully been introduced. This will even be true for the LDCs which, under a better adjustment process, should be less exposed to external imbalance and therefore more ready to distinguish between liquidity reserves and investment funds.

Even before the birth of the SDRs, plans had been suggested by which the Fund would be given the status of an international superbank with the power to create international money in much the same way in which national central banks increase the monetary circulation via lending or open-market operations. Robert Triffin suggested that an expanded IMF should be able to take the initiative and increase the liquidity reserves of LDCs in the form of Fund deposits via purchases of securities in the open market of these countries.[6] A different proposal by Maxwell Stamp would have let the IMF buy bonds issued by the International Development Association with newly created Fund certificates, which would then be used to finance the deficits of developing countries.[7]

These and other similar plans had in common that the supply of international liquidity would be consciously determined by an international central bank and would directly or indirectly be connected with the financing of development aid. Critics of these proposals, however, were quick to point to two difficulties: that the scheme would somehow have to be shielded against unlimited demands for development finance, a criticism which was answered with the suggestion that the total amount of liquidity creation per year should be strictly limited; and that the IOUs of poor countries, bought either directly, or indirectly via the IDA, would be considered poor "backing" behind the newly issued international money, while the IOUs of rich countries might be better backing but would increase the liquidity reserves of the wrong countries. The second point is important only if backing via IOUs is meant to support some form of value guarantee for newly issued liquidity reserves. Important is the fact that the conscious creation of an optimum amount of unconditional liquidity reserves must be protected against the danger of having the optimum miscalculated and voted for on the basis of development criteria that have nothing to do with international-payments problems.

The distinction between development finance and liquidity creation, however, need not make us reject the idea that, somehow, the seigniorage profit from international liquidity creation could be made available in toto for development finance. This could be done, for instance, if the original distribution of SDRs did not follow the members' quotas, or if the rich surplus countries were expected to lend their newly allocated SDRs to the IDA.

The attitude of the LDCs concerning the par-value system is conditioned by the following facts. First, many LDCs have a tendency to use trade and exchange controls rather than parity adjustments to achieve external balance. The major reason is the mixed character of their economic systems. They rely less on resource allocation through the pricing process than do the more advanced industrial countries. If resources are domestically allocated without much reference to price fluctuations it seems natural that the same process should be applied internationally, with the intention of protecting domestic planning against external uncertainties. The LDCs often blame their economic problems on the trade cycles in the industrial countries, and are not sure that the gains from international trade outweigh the losses from foreign-induced instability.

This attitude, while containing an element of truth—particularly in the light of the experiences of the interwar period—tends to forget that economic instability in the LDCs is, in the main, a product of their mixed economic system which is neither guided by a reliable pricing process nor by an all-inclusive central plan. Unrealistic price fixing and the setting of wrong priorities lead to misallocations of productive resources, while much administrative skill is wasted in managing control systems that are easily circumvented.

To these difficulties must be added the effects of excessive inflation, plus the political reluctance to adjust par values. Inflation results, among other causes, from welfare programs the LDCs cannot afford, and overvalued parities are defended with the argument that devaluation would only lead to further inflation via increasing import prices. The combination of domestic inflation and fixed par values leads to deficits that cannot be financed out of liquidity reserves. The latter are, as a rule, too small, owing to the desire to reduce liquidity in favor of investment. And lacking liquidity leads to even more stringent controls.

The LDCs are often wrong when they blame their difficulties predominantly on their external relations. International-payments problems can only be overcome if realistic parities are being used, that is, when prompt devaluations compensate for excessive inflationary developments. For LDCs that are not centrally planned, the arguments for realistic parities are basically the same as for other market economies.

If it were true that economic instability of the LDCs is mainly the result of fluctuations in their trade with the more-developed countries, then the most "open" LDCs would be the most unstable. Ronald I. McKinnon has found, however, that LDCs

were, on the average, about twice as unstable as mature industrial economies. . . . Hence, if business fluctuations originate mainly in the mature economies, and not in the LDCs themselves, somehow these fluctuations would have to be magnified when they are transmitted in order for the international economy to be a destabilizing influence.[8]

The presumption is that the international payments difficulties of the LDCs arise from their chronic tendency to overspend, together with unrealistic price-fixing and cumbersome controls. As far as international payments are concerned, a system with frequent par-value adjustments to domestic inflationary developments would be the better approach.

Endemic Inflation and Exchange-Rate Flexibility

Less-developed countries that are exposed to endemic inflation seem barred from joining an international-payments system with managed floating or frequent devaluations. The argument is as follows. In case of endemic inflation there is no doubt at all about the direction in which the par value will have to move. The tendency, therefore, would be to get rid of the domestic currency. And capital flight, in turn, would accelerate the depreciation process, unless par values were kept officially fixed. Countries with endemic inflation, accordingly, will have no choice but to freeze their par values and to achieve balance-of-payments equilibrium via payments and trade controls. Furthermore, it is generally assumed that payments systems with flexible exchange rates would strengthen already existing inflationary trends. In giving up the discipline of fixed parities, the developing countries would lose their last incentive to withstand inflation.

These arguments for fixed par values in countries with endemic inflation are wrong in spite of their superficial appeal. To begin with, the forces behind endemic inflation are far too strong to be brought under control by fixed parities and monetary policies needed in maintaining them. The result will only be that, as long as external equilibrium cannot be achieved via frequent parity adjustments or managed floating, a solution will be attempted by a further stiffening of controls. To already existing price and wage controls that are to repress domestic price inflation will be added payments and trade restrictions. Multiple exchange rates will be used to promote import substitution. But price, wage, and exchange controls have in common that they lead to misallocations of resources and to fundamental disequilibria which, eventually, will make substantial parity adjustments inevitable. These large adjustments, however, have shocklike effects and produce disequilibrating capital flows with economic consequences far exceeding those of frequent and small parity changes.

Controls are imposed in the belief that in times of major disturbances market forces cannot be trusted. The truth, however, is that the working of market forces opens a far better escape than the attempt to multiply controls—even if price inflation persists. In the case of inflation, *open* inflation is in the long run better than *repressed* inflation. In international payments this argues for a system in which par values are continuously adjusted to the waning purchasing power of the currency unit.

Recent experiences in Brazil have substantiated these theoretical conclusions.[9] Up to 1968 Brazil used various forms of exchange control to achieve external equilibrium in the face of sharply rising domestic prices and overvaluation of the cruzeiro. Waste, inefficiency, and black markets resulted and controls proliferated. In August 1968 the cruzeiro was devalued and it was decided that henceforth a new mini-devaluation policy would be followed. Between August 1968 and September 1, 1971, for instance, there were twenty-four devaluations averaging 1.6 percent in nominal terms and occurring on an average of every forty-four days.[10] These mini-devaluations eliminated the uncertainty and risk that had been characteristic for the large and relatively rare devaluations under the par-value system. The crawling-peg approach to devaluation, "coupled with a policy of maintaining positive real interest rates," [11] succeeded in eliminating the disequilibrating speculation that was characteristic for the system as long as par-values were artificially maintained.

The encouraging new feature in the Brazilian case of endemic inflation is the device of "monetary correction," which, through different types of escalator clauses, manages to offer a certain amount of protection against price inflation. Savings, for instance, not only earn interest, but are, in addition, protected against price inflation by a monetary correction equal to the rate of inflation. In a similar manner, mini-devaluation maintains realistic exchange rates. Under this system it becomes possible to avoid disequilibrating capital movements through adjustment of domestic real rates of interest to the mini-devaluations.

Brazilian experiences with mini-devaluation under conditions of endemic inflation contradict all the dire predictions concerning the inflationist effects of flexible exchange rates. Far from stimulating inflation, the new payments policy has not only helped reduce the rate of inflation, but has also permitted the price system to allocate domestic and foreign resources more economically than the previous system with its proliferation of controls.

10 Prospects

The Committee of Twenty and the Par-Value System

In June 1974 the IMF Committee on Reform of the International Monetary System, the so-called Committee of Twenty, published an *Outline of Reform.*[1] The main weakness of the *Outline* lies in the fact that the members of the Committee have tried to hold on to an international monetary system which is still to be based "on stable but adjustable par values," that is, on the old Bretton Woods formula. This is not surprising, since the guidelines set for the Committee contained the request that "attention should be directed to the appropriate monetary means and division of responsibilities for defending stable exchange rates." It was not made clear what the exchange rates were to be defended against.

A system with stable but adjustable par values cannot condone the floating exchange rates that we have today, and cannot operate under widely diverging rates of inflation in the member countries as they prevail at the moment. It is understandable, then, that the Committee of Twenty felt that the time had not yet come for a second Bretton-Woods type conference that would once more firmly establish the principle of stable but adjustable par values. It was decided, therefore, to switch for the time being "to a more evolutionary process of reform and to concentrate on those aspects that were most relevant to the present situation." [2]

Nevertheless, in spite of its basic weakness of aiming in the wrong direction, the *Outline of Reform* contains many valuable suggestions, especially in areas that are not directly connected with the adjustment problem.

The Committee has tried to improve the adjustment mechanism through somewhat greater flexibility of exchange rates, though the gliding or crawling band is not even mentioned and the "Guidelines for Floating" are vague and inconsistent. However, against these disappointing features we can hold the valuable recommendation that a new council in the Fund should constantly keep track of the adjustment process on the basis of objective criteria. What form the adjustment process is to take is not made clear. While the *Outline* discusses in some detail the "exchange rate mechanism" (paragraphs 11 to 13), and states that "there shall be a strong presumption against the use of controls on current account transactions or payments" (paragraph 14), insistence on stable par values and reluctance to permit frequent and small parity adjustments imply that the member countries are first and foremost expected to integrate their monetary policies. In other words, adjustment should, preferably, be brought about by monetary policies rather than by exchange-rate flexibility, since the latter is clearly opposed to stable par values.

The Committee of Twenty proposes the creation of "a permanent and representative Council," which, together with the Executive Board of the Fund, will oversee the adjustment process (paragraphs 31 and 5), and whose working will be largely based on the use of reserve indicators. "Countries will aim to keep their official reserves within limits which will be internationally agreed from time to time in the Fund" (paragraph 4).

Annexes 1 and 2 of the *Outline* make interesting suggestions concerning the operation of an "adjustment mechanism" based on objective indicators. These recommendations have to do with the definition of reserves and liabilities, target reserve levels, and a point system for the activation of the adjustment process. The basic idea is that the official reserves of the members should neither rise too high above nor fall too far below a proper reserve target. As the reserves move away from the target, they would pass, first, a "consultation point," then a point at which a country would become subject to "examination," and, finally, points at which it would be exposed to increasing "pressures."

For pressures that could be applied to countries *in surplus,* several interesting suggestions are made, namely: (1) "a charge on reserve accumulations above a reserve norm . . . graduated with respect to the size of the reserve accumulation and the duration of the imbalance"; (2) depositing "of reserves above a specified level with an Excess Reserve Account to be established in the Fund at zero interest"; (3) withholding of future SDR allocations; (4) a report on the external position and policies of the country; and finally, (5) the suggestion that "countries could be authorized to apply discriminatory trade and other current account restrictions against countries in persistent large surplus."

Countries *in deficit* could also be subjected to charges "graduated with respect to the size of the deficiency," interest rates on borrowings from the Fund could be raised, access to the resources of the Fund restricted, and future SDR allocations withheld. These pressures on deficit countries, though symmetrically conceived, make much less sense than the pressures to be applied to surplus countries. However, we have to remember that they are to be applied only when a member refuses to take proper steps in the form of devaluation. Since deficit countries are less likely to delay such adjustments than surplus countries a corresponding upvaluation, Annexes 1 and 2 of the *Outline* are important particularly with regard to the symmetry of the adjustment process that has been lacking in the Bretton Woods system. The proposals of the Committee combine valuable older suggestions, from Keynes's negative rate of interest on credit balances in the Clearing Union [3] to Donald Marsh's fixed reserve standard.[4] It is important to remember, though, that the Committee is not always thinking of *parity* adjustments. It would be a great step forward if the point system of the *Outline* were to be directly connected with frequent but small parity changes.

Annex 2 of the *Outline* distinguishes three methods of activation for the already mentioned pressure system; activation by positive Fund decision," "presumptive activation," and "automatic activation."

Reserve movements are not the only sign that adjustment might be needed. The Committee of Twenty considers it possible that "there is prima facie evidence that a country is facing significant imbalance, even though it is not indicated by a disproportionate movement in its reserves" (paragraph 6). We remember that already the Bretton Woods experts tried to make it clear that fundamental disequilibrium need not refer to the external balance only, since balance-of-payments equilibrium could be achieved at the cost of mass unemployment, imported inflation, or payments restrictions. It has become extremely unlikely by now, however, that member countries would go out of their way in their domestic monetary policies in order to maintain external balance at stable parities, merely to stay close to a reserve norm. There is no reason, then, why market forces should be prevented from affecting the liquidity reserves, and why changes in the latter should not be directly connected, via the point system, with parity adjustments.

In its discussion of the "exchange rate mechanism," the Committee of Twenty points out that "the exchange rate mechanism will be based on stable but adjustable par values," and insists that "countries should not make inappropriate par value changes. On the other hand, countries should, whether in surplus or deficit, make appropriate par value changes promptly." The suggestion that "the Fund may establish simplified procedures for approving small par value changes under appropriate safeguards" (paragraph 11) is not spelled out. Since the executive directors suggested earlier that changes in par values might be permitted "without concurrence of the Fund, as long as such changes do not exceed 3 percent per year," [5] we could perhaps be tempted to read more into the Committee's suggestion than was intended. But if we are not entitled to such a liberal interpretation, the *Outline* does, in fact, not support the operation of a gliding band, and must be criticized for backsliding in the direction of greater rigidity of exchange rates. Unfortunately, this interpretation is supported by the *Outline*'s guidelines for floating, as will be shown below.

The Committee of Twenty follows the example of the executive directors in speaking, inconsistently, of an exchange-rate mechanism while strongly supporting stable par values. The latter are, by definition, not market prices—they are prices that are artificially stabilized through intervention by monetary authorities in the exchange markets. In a real price mechanism prices change continuously under the impact of varying demand and supply conditions. In a system with stable par values, the market functions only to the extent that exchange rates are permitted to fluctuate within set margins around a central par value. A change of these central values by the monetary authorities, and with the permission of the Fund, cannot properly be called mechanical, particularly if an "automatic activation" of par-value changes on the basis of objective criteria (such as reserve levels) should be ruled out.

The *Outline* states that "except when authorized to adopt floating rates" countries will undertake the obligation to maintain specified maximum exchange rate margins for their currencies (paragraph 12). The Committee of Twenty obviously still thinks in terms of the order of magnitude of the margins established in December 1971 at the Smithsonian Conference, namely, 2¼ percent on either side of par, but suggests ways by which it may become possible for a country such as the United States, whose money is used as intervention currency, to participate equally in the flexibility that other countries enjoy on the basis of a broadened band. Unfortunately, the Committee of Twenty has neglected to discuss or recommend a further widening of the band or a gliding band, that is, the combination of a broadened band with a crawling peg. This is particularly disappointing in view of the fact that the "guidelines for floating" are the weakest part of the *Outline*.

The Committee of Twenty suggests that "countries should, whether in surplus or in deficit, make appropriate par value changes promptly" (paragraph 11). But the terms "appropriate" and "prompt" are left entirely vague, and opinions seem to differ still as widely as when Keynes and White disagreed thirty years ago.

The events of 1973 and 1974 forced upon the Committee of Twenty a more tolerant attitude concerning floating. Had widespread floating not occurred, it seems quite possible that the Committee would have ruled it out altogether. The existing situation forced the Committee of Twenty into grudging acceptance of floating "under special circumstances." The *Outline* states that "countries may adopt floating, subject to Fund authorization, surveillance and review" (paragraph 13). A closer study of the guidelines for floating in Annex 4 shows a disappointing lack of understanding of the importance of exchange-rate flexibility in the adjustment process.

The members of the Committee of Twenty were not in agreement as to whether the mere willingness to follow the guidelines for floating would already entitle a member to float its currency, or whether specific authorization by the Fund is needed. Recent events make this distinction look rather academic. We know that there is little the Fund can do if a member decides on floating.

Unfortunately, the Committee was not willing to connect its interesting suggestions concerning reserve criteria and a point system with its guidelines for floating, even though this connection suggests itself strongly and logically. Instead, we are told that a member may act "to moderate movements in the exchange value of its currency from month to month and quarter to quarter, and is encouraged to do so, if necessary, where factors recognized to be temporary are at work." This is an attempt to turn a system of managed floating back into a par-value system, an attempt exposed to the danger of the belated and large parity changes that were typical for the recent past and led to international monetary crises and the need for a thorough reform.

However, the experts are not even satisfied with exchange-rate stability that extends only over a few quarters. *Thinking in periods as long as four years,* they consider it desirable "to the extent that it is possible to form a reasonable estimate of the medium-term norm of a country's exchange rate, to resist movements in market rates that appear to be deviating substantially from that norm." [6] While such a policy is recommended by the Committee of Twenty particularly as safeguard against competitive exchange depreciation, it must be remembered that the far greater danger lies today in the permanent undervaluation of surplus currencies.

It would be desirable to consider far shorter periods than four years for the management of floating if we want to create a system in which exchange-rate adjustments can be activated on the basis of objective criteria. The signals emanating from variations in reserve assets should be substituted for the overly ambitious and abortive attempt to find out which market forces may or may not reverse themselves.

The Committee of Twenty seems to have grave doubts about its own guidelines for floating, for the latter are to take into account

that national policies, including those relating to domestic stabilization, should not be subjected to greater constraints than are clearly necessary in the national interest; . . . that a degree of uncertainty necessarily attaches to any estimate of a medium-term normal exchange rate, that this uncertainty is particularly great in present circumstances, and that on occasion the market view may be more realistic than any official view whether of the country primarily concerned or of an international body;

and that it may, therefore, at times be unavoidable "to forego or curtail official intervention that could be desirable from the standpoint of exchange stability if such intervention should involve an excessive drain on reserves or an impact on the money supply which is difficult to neutralize." [7]

Would it, then, not be far better to forget about medium-term intervention and, instead, connect changes in objective reserve indicators with exchange-rate adjustments either by managed floating or by way of a gliding band?

Toward an SDR Standard

While the *Outline of Reform* is relatively weak in its suggestions concerning the adjustment process, it tries consistently to promote reforms that, if successful, would establish an SDR standard and remove the difficulties that were connected with gold and the U.S. dollar as the major reserve assets.

In the interrelated question of convertibility and settlement, the Committee of Twenty aims at "symmetry of obligations for all countries including those whose currencies are held in official reserves. . . . All countries maintaining par values will settle in reserve assets official balances of their currencies which are presented to them for conversion" (paragraphs 18 and 20).

It may seem redundant that the *Outline* distinguishes between conversion and settlement, since settlement is nothing but the act of converting, that is, paying one's international obligations with generally acceptable reserve assets. That conversion and settlement are distinguished must be explained by the desire to treat the United States and other key-currency countries exactly like other members of the system. The United States, though maintaining market convertibility for the dollar, has not been "settling." Instead it has made use of its automatic borrowing rights, which derive from the quality of the dollar as intervention currency in the exchange markets. To add "settlement" to "conversion" probably means to say that in the case of countries such as the United States, whose currencies are held as official reserve assets, arrangements should be made to preclude such automatic borrowings and the continuing piling-up of foreign-held dollar or other key-currency balances in the future. These endeavors point to the desire to eliminate the dollar standard and to avoid the emergence of any other national currency as standard money. They imply, however, also that we must deal with the dollar overhang, that is, with the past accumulation of undesired dollar balances. Unless the dollar overhang is dealt with we cannot achieve what the *Outline of Reform* requests, namely, that "the aggregate volume of official currency holdings be kept under international surveillance and management by the Fund" (paragraph 19).

It is suggested, therefore, that

the Fund will, as necessary, make provisions for the consolidation of reserve currency balances to protect the future convertibility system against net conversion of any overhang of such balances which may exist at the restoration of general convertibility, and to ensure that the issuers of the currencies concerned will be able to acquire reserve assets when in surplus and will not lose reserve assets beyond the amount of any future official settlements deficits [paragraph 22].

The Committee of Twenty urges with good reason the future abandonment of the dollar standard, and tries to establish a system in whose advantages and costs all members participate in symmetrical fashion. For this purpose the *Outline* makes the constructive suggestion that a substitution account be established in the Fund that "will permit countries that wish to do so to exchange official currency holdings for SDRs" (paragraph 22).

The creation of a substitution account would be a big step in the direction of making the SDR the "principal reserve asset" (paragraph 24). If the Fund is to "allocate and cancel SDRs so as to ensure that the volume of global reserves is adequate" (paragraph 25), the Fund must not only be able to assess global reserve needs properly. It must also have first solved the problem of haphazard liquidity creation via growing dollar balances or changing policies toward the international role of gold. Once these preconditions for an SDR standard are met, it will still be necessary to groom the SDR for its new role as main reserve asset and international numéraire.

These arrangements will take much time and cooperation before they can be worked out properly. Part II of the *Outline of Reform,* dealing with "immediate steps," says only that "the Fund will give consideration to substitution arrangements." However, the suggestions made in Part I and in annexes 5 and 7 project potential future developments.

Annex 5 deals with "control over the aggregate volume of official currency holdings." It suggests that "the Fund would periodically agree on appropriate levels for the official liabilities in domestic currency of countries whose currencies had a significant reserve role." If, for instance, official foreign-held dollar balances increased beyond this agreed level, the United States, as "the issuing country, would redeem the increase by transferring reserve assets in exchange for its own currency."

Annex 7 discusses the creation of the substitution account, "through which SDRs may be issued in exchange for reserve currencies." The substitution account would be extremely helpful during the transition from a dollar to an SDR standard. It could, first of all, mop up the dollar overhang by changing official foreign dollar balances into SDR. Second, and in the future, the account could help achieve the Fund's aim of controlling the total amount of international liquidity reserves and the pattern of reserve asset composition. Member countries might be able to exchange excess accretions of U.S. dollar balances (or other major currencies) into SDRs; and the United States, in turn, would be permitted to buy SDRs with dollars to the extent that the foreign-held official dollar balances would fall below an agreed level.

It is important to note that "countries would not however be able to acquire currency balances in exchange for SDRs from the Substitution Account." The account would greatly strengthen the SDRs vis-à-vis dollar balances, and promote the aim that "the SDR will become the principal reserve asset and the role of gold and reserve currencies will be reduced" (paragraph 24).

In the working out of the details of the SDR standard, consideration will have to be given to the relaxation of existing constraints in the use of SDRs. The *Outline* makes suggestions concerning the limits on acceptance, the restitution provision, the limitations on SDR use, and similar restrictions that must be removed before the SDR can become the principal reserve asset.

Other considerations will have to deal with interest rates on SDR balances and the protection of the capital value of the SDR unit against depreciation (paragraph 26). We have already seen that the Fund has put into operation a standard basket valuation of the SDR.[8] Annex 9 of the *Outline* considers the problem further. It suggests, for instance, the possibility of giving the SDR a gradually increasing capital value by introducing "regular, small and uniform increases in the amount of each currency in the basket," pointing out "that the effect of the resulting appreciation in the capital value of the SDR on its total yield could be offset by a corresponding reduction in the interest rate."

Full control over the interest rate paid on SDR balances and over the latter's capital value should make it possible for the Fund to make the SDR the most desirable asset for reserve (but not hoarding) purposes, and promote its growing ascendancy over gold and balances in national currencies.

Concerning gold the *Outline of Reform* has not much to say. We are told that "appropriate arrangements will be made for gold, in the light of the agreed objectives that the SDR should become the principal reserve asset and that the role of gold should be reduced" (paragraph 28). In other words, gold will be internationally demonetized over the long run. In the short run, however, gold has still a major role to play. Gold reserves are at present "an important component of global liquidity" and "they should be usable to finance balance of payments deficits" (paragraph 28).

Obviously, the members of the Committee of Twenty have not been able to come to an agreement concerning the valuation of gold or the future of the still existing two-tier arrangement. The *Outline* mentions several possibilities.

Under one approach, monetary authorities, including the Fund, would be free to sell, but not to buy, gold in the market at the market price; they would not undertake transactions with each other at a price different from the official price, which would be retained and would not be subject to a uniform increase. Under another approach, the official price of gold would be abolished and monetary authorities, including the Fund, would be free to deal in gold with one another on a voluntary basis and at mutually acceptable prices, and to sell gold in the market. A third approach would modify the preceding one by authorizing monetary authorities also to buy gold in the market. Arrangements have also been proposed whereby the Fund would be authorized to purchase gold from monetary authorities in exchange for SDRs at a price between the market and the official price, and to sell gold gradually over time in the market; if arrangements of this kind were introduced, questions would arise concerning both the Fund's policy with respect to its sales in the market, and the sharing of any profits or losses accruing to the Fund from its gold transactions [par. 28].

None of these suggestions points to a return to gold in a crucially important international role, or to the likelihood of a massive upvaluation of gold as simple solution of the world's liquidity problem.

The *Outline*'s inclination to strengthen the SDR in comparison with the dollar and gold can, at least in part, be explained by the influence of the representatives of the less-developed countries on the Committee of Twenty. The LDCs are eager to establish a reformed international monetary system that will "promote an increasing net flow of real resources to developing countries" (paragraph 29). For this reason, "the possibility of establishing a link between development assistance and SDR allocation in the context of the reform has closely been examined." No agreement has been reached, but the *Outline* declares firmly that "if a link were to be established, the amount of SDR allocations and principal characteristics of SDRs should continue to be determined solely on the basis of global monetary requirements" (Annex 10).

The Impact of the Oil Crisis

It is remarkable that the great shock that was administered to the world economy by the sudden quadrupling of the price of crude oil did not create an international-payments crisis. The system of floating exchange rates was able to absorb the impact. It would be wrong, though, to conclude that flexible exchange rates can single-handedly solve the enormous new transfer problem that the world is now facing.

We should remember that in the twenties and thirties the world economy was much disturbed by the German reparations, their financing through private foreign lending, and the eventual breakdown of the transfer effort —a breakdown that helped bring Hitler to power. The new transfer problem, connected with the oil crisis, is much more pervasive than the old one was and may, if not very carefully handled, be even more destructive. It consists of several subproblems. First of all, it constitutes an enormous reshuffling of world income in favor of the oil-exporting countries and their cartel, the OPEC (Organization of Petroleum Exporting Countries), and at the expense of the oil-importing countries, which include highly industrial nations as well as poor developing countries. The oil importers will have to reduce their consumption drastically and for a very long time to be able to produce the vast export surpluses needed to transfer their oil payments.

The second part of the new transfer problem consists of the fact that most, if not all, oil-exporting countries find it utterly impossible to spend all their sudden new riches on additional imports. Their absorption capacity is limited by their sparse population, by the underdeveloped state of their economy, and by the intrinsic slowness of the development process. Since the oil-exporting countries cannot spend a major portion of their foreign earnings, they have no choice but to leave them in the oil-importing countries as some form of credit. The total balance of payments of all the oil-importing countries together will therefore, technically, remain in balance.

However, this technical overall balance hides a third major problem, since what is true for the aggregate does not apply to the individual oil-importing country whose deficit is not necessarily or automatically financed by the OPEC countries. All we can hope is that the world's financial system should somehow channel the OPEC's short-term balances to those oil importers who are in greatest need of them. As a matter of fact, this very thought must be behind the glib expression that the oil funds are being "recycled"—an unfortunate term that tends to hide some very intricate and serious international-payments difficulties. The fact is that this recycling involves a great deal of international monetary cooperation and can, if not carefully handled, destroy the whole international-payments system.

The sums that for lack of an alternative are held in terms of short-term credit instruments are enormous. In 1974 they amounted to probably 55 to 60 billion dollars. The OPEC countries will, of course, see to it that their foreign balances will offer the best combination of return and protection against depreciation. Unfortunately, however, the oil-consuming countries that offer the safest short-term investment opportunities are by no means the ones that need these funds most urgently to finance their balance-of-payments deficits. Furthermore, purely economic considerations do not tell the full story. We have always to remember the political nuisance value of disequilibrating shifts of short-term funds for the OPEC cartel.

In the very long run, the trade and payments problems of both importers and exporters of oil may be brought closer to a solution through the development of new energy resources by the importers and the economic development of the OPEC countries, so that they are enabled to absorb a larger portion of their surplus in terms of goods and services. For the short run, however, it is absolutely necessary to shift substantial amounts of the short-term balances of the OPEC countries into long-term investments in those oil-importing nations which need them most.

Basically, and in the long run, the oil importers must reduce the amount of their consumption by the equivalent of the OPEC countries' increased claims on their economies. This effort toward a reallocation of the world's productive resources may have inflationary and deflationary effects. The inflationary effects are due to the fact that these reallocations are supposed to be accomplished through the pricing process. Since downward adjustments of prices and wages are far harder to achieve than upward adjustments, it is almost certain that the outcome will be inflationary. The deflationary effects result from the fact that domestic consumption in the oil-importing countries will be sharply reduced, with no guarantee that increased demand by the OPEC countries will compensate for this shortfall. To avoid unemployment, the oil-importing countries will have to use fiscal policies. But while government deficit spending may maintain employment, the danger exists that employment creation becomes the primary aim and is, perhaps, accomplished through an expansion of domestic consumption demand where we had to start from the assumption that a reduction in the consumption level was the first step in a successful transfer process.

We can, therefore, consider a reduction of consumption only as successfully accomplished when the productive resources that have been set free are then used in the production of investment goods which, in the long run, will produce an export surplus for transfer purposes.

Another "key question concerns the extent to which the huge volume of capital flowing directly or indirectly from the oil exporting countries will mesh with the current account deficits of individual oil importing countries." [9] This meshing does not take place automatically; it must either happen as a reaction to price changes or it must be planned through international financial cooperation. Unless this problem is solved, the danger exists that we shall fall back into a situation in which each country fights for itself with beggar-my-neighbor policies.

The authorities of the International Monetary Fund are aware of the problem. In discussing "convertibility, consolidation and management of currency reserves," the *Outline of Reform* states expressly that "in this connection the Fund will take account . . . of the special position of a limited number of countries with large reserves deriving from depletable resources and with a low capacity to absorb imports." [10] Obviously, these countries will not be forced to upvalue their currencies whenever their official reserves exceed a norm that would be normal under other circumstances. However, it will be impossible for the Fund to limit its efforts in the long run to *official* currency balances. Considering the enormous growth of the Eurocurrency market, its capacity to multiply deposits by a process of credit creation,[11] and the inflationary potential of this situation of excessive liquidity, the time has come to try to draw these funds into the consolidation effort of the IMF.

Both the Fund and the Bank have already made efforts to solve the international financial problems caused by the quadrupling of the price of oil.

The Fund announced on June 13, 1974 the creation of an

oil facility under which resources will be made available to member countries to assist them to meet the impact on the balance of payments of increases in the cost of petroleum and petroleum products. Resources made available under this decision will be supplementary to any assistance that members may obtain under other policies on the use of the Fund's resources.[12]

These credits are conditional. First, the Fund must be satisfied that the member needs the assistance because the cost of oil has increased its deficit. Second, the member must cooperate with the Fund in finding "appropriate solutions for its balance of payments problem." Third, the loan must be repaid as soon as possible "and in any event in sixteen quarterly instalments to be completed not later than seven years after the purchase." [13] Fourth, since the interest on Fund borrowings will be at an annual rate of 7 percent, "corresponding rates would be charged to members that draw under the facility." [14] Fifth, and finally, the borrowing countries "must not adopt policies which would merely aggravate the problems of other countries." [15] In other words, they have to avoid competitive depreciation and the escalation of restrictions on trade and payments.

In chapter 9 we saw that it is important that the functions of the International Monetary Fund and the World Bank be clearly distinguished, because the Fund deals with short-term resources which must be kept liquid while the World Bank should take care of long-term investments in developing countries. However, the problems connected with the oil crisis suggest that both institutions can cooperate, with the Fund helping to transform short-term into medium-term balances and the Bank trying to borrow as much as possible from OPEC earnings and investing these sums in the economies of the developing countries that need them most. The World Bank has already made good progress in this role as intermediary between the OPEC and the oil-importing developing countries.

The oil crisis has superimposed grave new problems on an already difficult international payments situation. The danger is great that individual oil-importing countries, in a nervous *sauve-qui-peut* attitude, will try to solve their difficulties by beggaring their neighbors. However, the risks inherent in the present situation are so obvious that they may actually create a climate for, and the will to, international monetary cooperation for the benefit of all. Even the OPEC countries must be interested in the economic health of the countries from which are to come the means for their own future development.

Only a well-working international payments mechanism with sufficiently flexible exchange rates will be able to accomplish the many delicate adjustments which are implied in the process of recycling and the eventual transfer of commodities and services to oil-exporting countries.

Notes

Chapter 2
Gold and Gold-Exchange Standard

1. Alvin H. Hansen, *Full Recovery or Stagnation?* (New York: W. W. Norton, 1938), p. 210.

2. John Maynard Keynes, Speech delivered before the House of Lords, May 23, 1944. Reprinted in Seymour E. Harris (ed.), *The New Economics: Keynes' Influence on Theory and Public Policy* (New York: Alfred A. Knopf, 1948).

3. Joan Robinson, *Introduction to the Theory of Employment* (London: Macmillan and Co., 1938), p. 110.

4. John Maynard Keynes, *Essays in Persuasion* (New York: Harcourt, Brace and Company, 1932), p. 250.

5. Alvin H. Hansen, *Fiscal Policy and Business Cycles* (New York: W. W. Norton, 1941), p. 99.

6. John Maynard Keynes, *The General Theory of Employment, Interest, and Money* (London: Macmillan and Co., 1936); Seymour E. Harris (ed.), *The New Economics,* op. cit., Part Five.

Chapter 3
The International Monetary Fund and the Dollar

1. *The White Plan:* Preliminary Draft Outline of a Proposal for an International Stabilization Fund for the United and Associated Nations (Revised July 10, 1943); *The Keynes Plan:* Proposals for an International Clearing Union (April 1943). Reprinted in *The International Monetary Fund 1945–1965,* Volume III *Documents* (International Monetary Fund, Washington, D.C., 1969), pp. 83–96, 19–36.

2. *Articles of Agreement of the International Monetary Fund* (July 22, 1944). Reprinted in *The International Monetary Fund 1945–1965,* Vol. III *Documents* (International Monetary Fund, Washington, D.C., 1969), pp. 185–214.

3. Speech delivered before the House of Lords, May 23, 1944. Reprinted in Seymour E. Harris (ed.), *The New Economics: Keynes' Influence on Theory and Public Policy* (New York: Alfred A. Knopf, 1948).

4. John H. Williams, "Currency Stabilization: the Keynes and White Plans," *Foreign Affairs,* July 1943, pp. 649–50.

5. The merit of having drawn attention to this problem belongs to Robert Triffin, *Gold and the Dollar Crisis. The Future of Convertibility* (New Haven, Conn.: Yale University Press, 1960).

Chapter 4
International Liquidity and Special Drawing Rights

1. See *International Monetary Arrangements: The Problem of Choice*. Report on the Deliberations of an International Study Group of 32 Economists (Princeton, N.J.: Princeton University, 1964), chapter 2.

2. The IMF has changed its unit of account from the U.S. dollar "as of July 1, 1944" to SDR, the unit of the Special Drawing Rights discussed below.

3. *The International Monetary Fund 1945–1965,* Vol. II *Documents* (Washington, D.C., 1969), p. 538.

4. Ibid., p. 18.

5. See Group of Ten, *Report of the Study Group on the Creation of Reserve Assets* (Ossola Report) of May 1965, chapter 3.

6. *Establishment of a Facility Based on Special Drawing Rights in the International Monetary Fund and Modifications in the Rules and Practices of the Fund* (April 1968). Reprinted in *The International Monetary Fund 1945–1965,* Vol. III *Documents* (Washington, D.C., 1969), pp. 497–541.

7. Fritz Machlup, *Remaking the International Monetary System: The Rio Agreement and Beyond* (Baltimore: The Johns Hopkins Press, 1968), p. 35.

Chapter 5
The Basic Weakness of the Par-Value System

1. *The Role of Exchange Rates in the Adjustment of International Payments*. A Report by the Executive Directors (International Monetary Fund: Washington, D.C., 1970); *Reform of the International Monetary System*. A Report by the Executive Directors to the Board of Governors (International Monetary Fund: Washington, D.C., 1972).

2. *The Role of Exchange Rates,* op. cit., p. 67.

3. Ibid., p. 6.

4. Ibid.

5. Ibid., p. 32.

6. Ibid.

7. Ibid., p. 34.

8. Ibid.

9. Ibid., p. 48.

10. Ibid., p. 49.

11. Ibid., p. 35.

12. Ragnar Nurkse, *Conditions of International Monetary Equilibrium,* Essays in International Finance, No. 4 (Princeton: Princeton University, 1945).

13. Milton Friedman, "The Case for Flexible Exchange Rates," in *Essays in Positive Economics* (Chicago: The University of Chicago Press, 1953), p. 184.

Chapter 6
The Gliding Band and Managed Floating

1. *The Role of Exchange Rates in the Adjustment of International Payments.* A Report by the Executive Directors (International Monetary Fund: Washington, D.C. 1970), p. 71.

2. Ibid., chapter 4.

3. See *Approaches to Greater Flexibility of Exchange Rates. The Bürgenstock Papers,* arranged by C. Fred Bergsten, George N. Halm, Fritz Machlup, and Robert V. Roosa (Princeton, N.J.: Princeton University Press, 1970), pp. vii–viii.

4. See George N. Halm, *The "Band" Proposal: The Limits of Permissible Exchange Rate Variations,* Special Papers in International Economics No. 6 (Princeton, N.J.: Princeton University, 1965).

5. See John H. Williamson, *The Crawling Peg,* Essays in International Finance No. 50 (Princeton, N.J.: Princeton University, 1965).

6. Stephen Marris, *The Bürgenstock Communiqué: A Critical Examination of the Case for Limited Flexibility of Exchange Rates,* Essays in International Finance No. 80 (Princeton, N.J.: Princeton University, 1970), pp. 62–63.

7. *The Role of Exchange Rates in the Adjustment of International Payments,* op. cit., p. 73.

8. See, for instance, *Approaches to Greater Flexibility,* op. cit., pp. 36, 228.

9. *Approaches to Greater Flexibility,* op. cit., pp. 54, 234, 240, 245–49.

10. Gottfried Haberler and Thomas D. Willett, *A Strategy for U.S.*

Balance of Payments Policy (Washington, D.C.: American Enterprise Institute, 1971), p. 13.

11. Richard N. Cooper, "Sliding Parities: A Proposal for Presumptive Rules," in *Approaches to Greater Flexibility, op. cit.,* pp. 251–59.

12. *Approaches to Greater Flexibility, op. cit.,* p. vii.

13. Harry G. Johnson, "The Case for Flexible Exchange Rates, 1969," in *Approaches to Greater Flexibility, op. cit.,* p. 101.

14. Fritz Machlup, "Exchange-rate Flexibility," in *Banca Nationale del Lavoro Quarterly Review* No. 106, September 1973.

15. Donald B. Marsh, "The Fixed-Reserve Standard: A Proposal to 'Reverse' Bretton Woods," in *Approaches to Greater Flexibility, op. cit.,* pp. 261–69.

16. Milton Friedman, Statement before the Subcommittee on International Exchange and Payments of the Joint Committee of the Congress, June 21, 1973.

Chapter 7
Which Standard: Gold, Dollar, or SDR?

1. For the best defense of gold see Don D. Humphrey, "The Case for Gold," in *Leading Issues in International Economic Policy,* C. Fred Bergsten and William G. Tyler, eds. (Lexington, Mass.: D. C. Heath and Company, Lexington Books, 1973), pp. 81–98.

2. Don D. Humphrey, op. cit.

3. Roy Harrod, *Reforming the World's Money* (New York: St. Martin's Press, 1965), chapter 3; Peter M. Oppenheimer, "The Outlook for the Present World Monetary System," in *Approaches to Greater Flexibility of Exchange Rates. The Bürgenstock Papers,* arranged by C. Fred Bergsten, George N. Halm, Fritz Machlup, and Robert V. Roosa (Princeton, N.J.: Princeton University Press, 1970), pp. 179–85.

4. Jacques Rueff, "Gold Exchange Standard a Danger to the West" and Michael A. Heilperin, "The Case for Going Back to Gold," in *World Monetary Reform. Plans and Issues,* ed. by Herbert G. Grubel (Stanford, Calif.: Stanford University Press, 1963), pp. 320–28, 329–42.

5. Milton Gilbert, *The Gold-Dollar System: Conditions of Equilibrium and the Price of Gold.* Essays in International Finance No. 70 (Princeton, N.J.: Princeton University, 1968); Don D. Humphrey, op. cit.

6. Letter to George N. Halm, quoted in Don D. Humphrey, op. cit.

7. Gottfried Haberler, "Prospects for the Dollar Standard," Lloyds Bank Review, No. 105, July 1972.

8. See *IMF Survey* of July 8, 1974.

9. Ibid.

10. Ibid.

11. Tom de Vries, *An Agenda for Monetary Reform,* Essays in International Finance No. 95 (Princeton, N.J.: Princeton University, 1972), p. 15.

12. William B. Dale, "The International Monetary Fund and Greater Flexibility of Exchange Rates," in *Leading Issues of International Economic Policy,* op. cit., p. 97.

Chapter 8
The European Monetary Union

1. Harry G. Johnson, "The Case for Flexible Exchange Rates, 1969," in *Approaches to Greater Flexibility of Exchange Rates. The Bürgenstock Papers,* arranged by C. Fred Bergsten, George N. Halm, Fritz Machlup, and Robert V. Roosa (Princeton, N.J.: Princeton University Press, 1970), p. 97.

2. Robert A. Mundell, *The International Monetary System: Conflict and Reform* (Quebec: The Canadian Trade Committee, 1965), chapter 5.

3. See, for instance, Antonio Mosconi in *Approaches to Greater Flexibility,* op. cit., p. 389.

4. Wolfgang Kasper, "European Integration and Greater Flexibility of Exchange Rates," in *Approaches to Greater Flexibility,* op. cit., pp. 385–87.

5. John Maynard Keynes, *Essays in Persuasion* (New York: Harcourt, Brace and Company, 1932), p. 245.

6. For a critical appraisal of the European Monetary Union see Herbert Giersch (ed.), *Integration Through Monetary Union* (Tübingen: I.C.B. Mohr, 1971); Hans Willgerodt and others, *Wege und Irrwege zur Europäischen Währungsunion* (Freiburg i.B.: Rombach, 1972).

7. Wolfgang E. Kasper and Heinz-Michael Stahl, *Integration Through Monetary Union—A Sceptical View,* Kieler Diskussionsbeiträge No. 7, Institut für Weltwirtschaft, Kiel 1970.

8. See *IMF Survey,* March 18, 1974.

Chapter 9
Less-Developed Countries

1. Gottfried Haberler, "Critical Observations on Some Current Notions in the Theory of Economic Development," in *Scritti in Onore di Guiseppe Ugo Papi* (Milano: Editrice L'Industria, 1957), p. 7.

2. International Bank for Reconstruction and Development, Articles of Agreement, 1944, Art. III-4.

3. International Bank for Reconstruction and Development, *Seventh Annual Report,* 1951–52.

4. Art. IV-4.

5. International Bank for Reconstruction and Development, *Fifteenth Annual Report,* 1959–60.

6. Robert Triffin, *Gold and the Dollar Crisis* (New Haven: Yale University Press, 1960).

7. Maxwell Stamp, "The Stamp Plan—1962 Version," in *Moorgate and Wallstreet* (Autumn 1962).

8. Ronald I. McKinnon, "The Monetary Approach to Exchange-Rate Policy in Less Developed Countries," in *Exchange Rate Policy in Southeast Asia,* Herbert C. Grubel and Theodore Morgan editors (Lexington, Mass.: D. C. Heath and Company, Lexington Books, 1973), p. 70.

9. See William G. Tyler, "Exchange Rate Flexibility under Conditions of Endemic Inflation: A Case Study of Recent Brazilian Experience," in *Leading Issues in International Economic Policy,* edited by C. Fred Bergsten and William G. Tyler (Lexington, Mass.: D. C. Heath and Company, Lexington Books, 1973), pp. 19–49.

10. Ibid., p. 22.

11. Ibid., p. 33.

Chapter 10
Prospects

1. *Outline of Reform with Accompanying Annexes, IMF Survey,* Vol. 3, No. 12, June 17, 1974, pp. 193–208.

2. See Address by Jeremy Morse, Ibid., p. 186.

3. See chapter 3 above.

4. See chapter 6 above.

5. See note 1 to chapter 6.

6. See "Guidelines for Management of Floating," *IMF Survey,* Vol. 3, No. 12, June 17, 1974, pp. 181–83.

7. Ibid.

8. See chapter 7 above.

9. Opening Statement by the Managing Director of the Fund to the 29th Annual Meeting in Washington on September 20, 1974. See *IMF Survey,* Vol. 3, No. 20, October 14, 1974, p. 325.

10. See *Outline of Reform,* paragraph 19.

11. For the best description of this process see Milton Friedman, "The Euro-Dollar Market: Some First Principles," *The Morgan Guarantee Survey,* October 1969, pp. 4–14.

12. *IMF Survey,* Vol. 3, No. 12, June 17, 1974, p. 177.

13. Ibid., p. 185.

14. Ibid.

15. Ibid., p. 186.

Index

Index

121

About the Author

George N. Halm is Emeritus Professor of Economics at the Fletcher School of Law and Diplomacy at Tufts University. He received the Ph.D. degree in 1924 at the University of Munich, Germany. Dr. Halm has published several books in German. His publications in English (and several foreign languages) include *Monetary Theory* (1942, 1946), *International Monetary Cooperation* (1945), *Economic Systems* (1951, 1960, 1968) and *Economics of Money and Banking* (1956, 1961).